◆ Praise for *Give Wings To Your Dreams*

"Lauren Sullivan leads by inspiring example, taking you on a soul-satisfying journey of personal discovery and freedom to recapture your dreams and celebrate the joy in your life."

– Sandy Grason,

Author of *Journalution, Journaling to Awaken Your Inner Voice, Heal Your Life and Manifest Your Dreams*

"Lauren Sullivan encourages women to explore their passion, take risks, listen to their inner guidance and take good care of themselves. She wisely reminds us that whatever we choose to do, success is measured in feeling happy, contented, at peace and loved. Through her own journey from lost to found, she imparts hope, enthusiasm and clear guidance to the reader for taking on the adventure called life."

– Charlotte Sophia Kasl, Ph.D.,

Author of *Many Roads, One Journey: Moving Beyond the Twelve Steps* and *If the Buddha Got Stuck: A Handbook for Change on a Spiritual Path*

"Lauren Sullivan courageously and openly tells her story and that of countless others. Full of rich metaphors and personal examples, it is a reminder of who we are, of giving and receiving, forgiveness and so much more. It provides an effective model for all who desire to reach inside and give wings to their own dreams. I plan to share this inspiring work of art with my clients."

– Margie S. Heiler, MS,

Master Certified and Certified Executive Coach

"Whether you are taking your first step on the path to self-discovery or you've been traveling the path for some time, you will find profound and insightful strategies in this wonderful book! Lauren's uplifting writing style, her rich, poignant stories, and her well crafted exercises give you the tools you need to discover your own personal pathway to a joyful life. After you've read the book, be sure to keep the summary of questions and activities close at hand because it is worth its weight in gold!"

– Carol McClelland, Ph.D.,
Author of *The Seasons of Change* and *Your Dream Career For Dummies*

"For too many women, dreams remain just that: elusive, out of reach, and unfulfilled. If you've lost faith or never quite connected with your own precious—or powerful—dreams, this book could be just what the magician ordered!"

– Daphne Rose Kingma,
Author of *Loving Yourself* and *Finding True Love*

"*Give Wings To Your Dreams* takes you on a gentle and compassionate journey, illuminating a path that will empower and energize you to spread your own wings and fly. A beautiful book."

– Susan Jeffers, Ph.D.,
Author of *Feel the Fear and Do It Anyway* and *Life is Huge!*

Give Wings to Your DREAMS

Reawaken Your Joy
and Passion for Life

Lauren E. Sullivan

$\mathcal{GW}$

Golden Wings Press
3905 State Street, Suite #7-292
Santa Barbara, CA 93105
Visit our website at
www.GoldenWingsPress.com

Cover and Interior Design by Toolbox Creative
Cover Art by Meganne Forbes
Author photo by Linda Blue

The author gratefully acknowledges the following permissions:

Paul J. Meyer quote. Reprinted with permission of Paul J. Meyer, The Meyer Resource Group, Inc., Waco, TX 76710.

Anaïs Nin quote. Permission to use this quotation granted by Barbara W. Stuhlmann, Author's Representative.

Laura Ingalls Wilder quote. From *A Little House Sampler* by Laura Ingalls Wilder and Rose Wilder Lane and edited by William T. Anderson. Copyright © 1988 by HarperCollins Publishers Inc. Reprinted by permission of HarperCollins Publishers.

Napoleon Hill quote. Courtesy Napolean Hill Foundation, www.naphill.org.

Margaret Lee Runbeck quote. © Estate of Margaret Lee Runbeck. Reprinted by permission of Harold Matson Co., Inc.

Gloria Steinem quote. Courtesy, Gloria Steinem.

ISBN 978-0-9778538-1-6
ISBN 0-9778538-1-0

◆ Dedication

To my husband, Eric Sullivan:

You are my rock, my wellspring of calm and loving energy, and my role model for living a balanced life. You have so generously and unconditionally offered your love and support, and given me the space to follow my dreams.

To my son Greg:

At eighteen, your wisdom and maturity is well beyond your years. You have more direction and clarity than most who are more than twice your age. I know your vision, your passion, and your drive to succeed will take you where you want to go!

To my son Kevin:

At sixteen, you have a rare combination of right-brain creativity and left-brain intellect. You are so full of inventive ideas and possibilities. You have so much to work with as you discover the direction in life that will make your heart sing!

◆Table of Contents

Part III:
Bringing Your Dreams Into Reality

"Whatever you vividly imagine, ardently desire, sincerely believe and enthusiastically act upon, must inevitably come to pass."

–Paul J. Meyer

The Journey To Where You Want To Be

Seven stepping stones that will transform your life

The butterfly is a universal symbol for transformation.
Emerging from its cocoon
with beautiful, colorful, multifaceted wings,
the butterfly transcends limitations encountered
in the past. So it can be for us, as we give wings to our dreams.

You've had thoughts and dreams about a new direction in life. Something calls to you. There is a relentless tug, a deep-rooted urge for something more, something better. You might be feeling you came here for a purpose, but what is it?

Perhaps your life has been thrown into chaos because a change was thrust upon you when you least expected it and you are feeling shell-shocked and confused. You have been grieving the loss of one dream, but you are beginning to have inklings of a new and better dream awakening.

Maybe it feels like you are standing at the precipice of what seems like the Grand Canyon. It is daunting indeed to look at the distance you must travel to get there from here. If only you had wings to get across to the other side to live your dream!

If you are experiencing turmoil in your life, take heart! Even though there seems to be a great divide between where you are today and where you want to be, you *can* take charge and transform your life. I know because I've been there and done that in my own life and I've helped many other women do the same.

What all dreams have in common is a desire to in some way improve the quality of our lives. The desire for a better quality of life is universal, yet few of us seem to know how to actually achieve it. The quest for quality of life, for work/life balance, for basic happiness and contentment with our lives can be an elusive and frustrating goal. Perhaps this is our modern-day Holy Grail.

Midlife crises used to be about men in their forties and fifties suddenly buying little red sports cars and reaching for youthful pleasures. In this equal opportunity world, the midlife crisis strikes women as often as men and what we are seeing is that a "midlife crisis" of burnout and confusion is hitting women as early as their thirties! We live our lives intensely. We all lament for more time in the day, more days in the week. If only we had the time, we'd find the way to start that new business, find our life partner, spend more time traveling to exotic places. If only we had more courage, we'd find the way to end a toxic relationship, change careers, write a book. If only we had the energy, we'd have a full, vibrant and joyful life!

All too often our important desires are relegated to the backburner. We live with our longings and frustrations for years on end without taking any significant action to satisfy the need. Why? Overwhelm, analysis paralysis, fear of the unknown, lack of focus, lack of time, confusion, and self-limiting beliefs are but a few of the forces that conspire to keep us stuck in our distress. It is sad that for many who have a dream of a better life, the journey ends before it has a chance to begin. But what if you could break through these obstacles and breathe life into your ideas, giving your dreams a place of honor and priority in your day-to-day life?

Give Wings To Your Dreams offers Seven Stepping Stones to guide you along your own personal journey from lost to found. These are stepping stones you can traverse at your own pace to make your journey manageable while you also attend to the demands of daily life. After all, you've still got bills to pay and laundry to do.

Transforming your life is not for the faint-of-heart! It is a journey that will require that you leave certain baggage behind, challenge old belief systems, and open to a new view of yourself. It will require you to believe that you can truly have what you want—and that you are worthy of having it! It will mean making a rock-solid commitment to yourself to follow your dream. And it will require patience and perseverance on your part as you plant the seeds of your future and nurture them to grow.

Depending on the magnitude of change you desire, you could experience results in a few weeks or months or it might take you a number of years to get where you want to be. It is important to gain a clear vision of where you want to go and then begin to take steps to achieve what you want. Even the smallest steps you begin today will give you momentum and the satisfaction that you are heading in the right direction. The good news is that baby steps over time add up to magnificent strides. We all have within us the power to spread our wings and fly to the destination of our choosing.

The purpose of this book is to illuminate the path that will empower you to create the quality of life you deeply desire! My intention is to give you tools to help you sort through options and obstacles and guide you to make powerful and productive life choices. The Seven Stepping Stones will propel you forward with confidence, clarity, and conviction and support you as you give wings to your dreams!

My Own Journey From Lost To Found

I came to this awareness of the Seven Stepping Stones offered in *Give Wings To Your Dreams* as a result of my own experience of traveling from lost to found. Today I am living on the beautiful California coast in Santa Barbara, working as a life coach, writing books, facilitating personal retreats, teaching workshops, and standing before large audiences giving inspirational speeches. I recently married a wonderful man who gives me his unconditional love and support and who adores my kids. My teenage boys respect and admire him and there is harmony in our home. I love my life. I'm feeling happy and fulfilled, doing work I love and making a difference. This has not always been the case. I went through an intense life upheaval on the way to living my dreams.

When I turned forty, I hit rock bottom and it was a long fall. I had reached the pinnacle of my career as a Silicon Valley marketing executive with worldwide responsibilities. It was exhilarating and exhausting. I was learning the ropes as a single mom as well, having recently separated from my husband of fourteen years. There's nothing extraordinary about this. It was stressful and demanding and not too different from the life of most working mothers. It's a tightrope act and as long as we don't get hit with a hurricane-force wind, we seem to manage to stay upright.

But life happens and sometimes it's not pretty. One day, a year or so into the separation from my husband, I returned late on a Sunday evening from a ski weekend in Tahoe. On

Monday morning, I checked my voicemail from the office and found a message from my ten-year-old son. He and his younger brother had been staying with their dad in San Francisco for the weekend. Their dad was to have driven them to school on Monday morning.

I froze in stunned horror when I listened to the message, "Mommy, please come get us!" my son pleaded. "Daddy didn't take us to school today. He's been busy building a machine to make the little man in his head stop talking." You should have seen me fly out the door and into my car. It was the longest hour of my life as I made the trip to San Francisco to get my kids out of there.

This was my rude awakening that something was seriously wrong with my husband. It was the beginning of a two-year horror show in which I became an unwitting central character. At first, I thought my husband had developed a mental illness or possibly a brain tumor. As his behavior became increasingly bizarre I learned that he had become hopelessly addicted to crystal meth, one of the most insidious, brain-frying, life-threatening drugs out there. He had become a danger to himself and others—particularly to my kids and me.

I lived in constant despair as my husband's behavior became increasingly unpredictable and dangerous. He would slip in and out of grandiose personas sincerely believing he was Alexander the Great or the Devil himself. He called me one night after an earthquake, distraught in his belief he had caused it. I vacillated between feeling pity for him and abject fear. There were frightening phone calls, threats, maniacal rages, and demands to take the children. There were late night calls to the sheriff and urgent advice for me to get a restraining order. I could not believe this was happening to me!

My husband had been my best friend. Though circumstances had led us down the path of divorce, we still cared for each other. I wanted desperately to rescue him, to get him the help he needed to beat his drug addiction. I didn't want my children to lose their father.

In my frantic attempts to rescue him, a therapist had told me that I was not only beating my head against the wall, I was putting myself in harm's way. He had said bluntly there were three possible outcomes for a meth addict: death, homelessness, or jail. In deep denial, I was certain there had to be another way.

One day I had a strong premonition that something was terribly wrong. I arranged for an intervention team to meet me at my husband's home in San Francisco. The plan had been to try to get him into a drug treatment program. When we arrived, what we found was a vision of madness, a man with wild eyes and unkempt hair who was extremely agitated. He very theatrically and graciously invited us up to his rooftop deck, appearing very excited to have an audience for some "ceremony" he was performing. He spoke of the importance of this ceremony; that he had called the President and the Pope because they would want to know. I exchanged wary glances with the mental health professionals I had brought with me. He offered us each a glass of wine and we followed him upstairs to the roof deck. There he reached for a loaded rifle!

Needless to say, as he grabbed the rifle, we all panicked, fled the building, and called 911. My husband had been distraught over the recent death of his father, a highly decorated army officer. In his drug-crazed, delusional mind, he was conducting a 21-gun salute to honor his father—in the middle of a densely populated residential neighborhood!

The police arrived on the scene instantly. I found myself cowering on the street corner as a SWAT team went thundering past me. Apparently the police had been looking for the source of intermittent gunfire in the neighborhood for several hours. I heard the police-band radio crackle, "We've got him in our sights." I looked up at the church rooftop on the corner and I could see the sharpshooter with his rifle aimed squarely at his target. I began to shiver and shake and cry hysterically. I was so afraid they were going to shoot him dead. It seemed my intentions for that day had totally backfired. I had come to rescue him. It appeared the police were intent on ending his misery.

Miraculously, the arrest was quick and without bloodshed. My husband emerged from the building battered, bruised, and handcuffed. A proud man, even in his deranged state, he belligerently and regally demanded they read his Miranda rights. Shaken to the core, I moved like a zombie as I was escorted to the police station, where my husband was booked and taken away to jail.

I can't begin to describe the numbness I felt in that moment, but it was very clear to me that our lives had changed forever. My husband, who had been a six-figure income earner with not so much as a traffic ticket on his record, found himself facing felony charges. I am convinced now that his going to jail was the best possible outcome. Incarceration is what saved his life.

My husband was eventually able to enter a treatment program and beat the incredible odds to overcome his drug addiction. Through great courage and conviction, and the passage of time, he has been able to transform his life. He has channeled his enormous creative talents into a business that is fun and satisfying for him.

We got our divorce and went our separate ways. My kids got their father back, though at a distance, and they maintain a loving relationship. My boys have first-hand knowledge of the pain of drug addiction and a steadfast commitment to steer clear of drugs. Though I would have never wished for them to learn it in this way, they have developed strength of character beyond their years.

Turning Turmoil Into Triumph

Throughout this ordeal I found myself in a complete fog, walking through a life that had become utterly surreal. My image of how life was supposed to be had shattered completely. I was immersed in feelings of extreme distress, confusion, hopelessness, helplessness, and deep despair. Life had to go on, and I struggled to stay afloat in the demanding world of Silicon Valley.

I had been a high achiever my entire career, but my two-year ordeal had taken its toll on my performance. I could not concentrate and I felt sick, tired, and worried all the time, yet I managed to keep going, to show up for work most days and get things done— just not nearly to the level at which I had become accustomed.

I had been putting on a mask each day to go to work, trying to act as if everything was okay. But everything was not okay. I had pushed myself beyond any reasonable limits to keep myself going, striving to be Superwoman. While I had managed to look pretty super on the outside for a while, I was looking pretty gnarly on the inside. The façade was beginning to crack. I was aware I was developing a reputation for being intense, uptight, edgy, and a bit flaky. I'm sure my team had some rather more colorful descriptors! There is no doubt I was losing it.

It is interesting how you can hold yourself reasonably together and push yourself to keep going during an extreme crisis—for a while. But when the danger passes, and you can relax, that's when you fall apart. That's how it happened for me.

My job involved worldwide travel. One day, I had booked tickets for a weeklong business trip to Japan when my body just said no. It was as if my body had chained itself to a post and dared me to do anything about it! It became clear that day that I could no longer soldier on. I had been running on empty for way too long and I had reached the point of no return. I simply had to stop the world and get off.

I had totally neglected my own well-being to the point I was now facing profound health issues. I was suffering from post-traumatic stress, chronic fatigue, and severe digestive problems. The stress and lack of attention to my own self-care had led me to a point of extreme burnout on life itself.

My doctor ordered a medical leave of absence from my job and those meetings in Japan went on without me. I embarked on the road back to my physical and emotional health and that was the beginning of my personal journey from lost to found.

I have come to see the gift in the adversity I experienced. Hitting rock bottom became the springboard that launched me on a path that revealed wonderful new possibilities for my life. I was able to reclaim my deepest desires and find the way to live the dreams I had long denied. Most of all, I was able to find joy again and a quality of life that had always seemed out of reach. Not only was I able to give wings to my own dreams, I discovered in doing so that my purpose in life is to help others do the same.

Okay, I confess. I was completely unable to see the gift in the horror I experienced at the time! There were plenty of days when I curled up in a little ball and pulled the covers over my head! Days when I felt like giving up, days when I felt lost and confused and even helpless and hopeless. I sank into depression at times, along with pity-parties, resentment, and rage. But some part of me was resilient enough to reach for hope, health, and a new direction.

I ran across a Dilbert cartoon once that summed it up for me. "That which does not suck the life force from you makes you stronger!" I kept that cartoon taped to my refrigerator for a long time. It gave me some comfort that there might be light at the end of the tunnel. And indeed there was. Yet mine was not an overnight transformation.

My journey took some years to get from rock bottom to a life that really works for me. The journey was not always in a straight line either. I've had some ups and downs along the way. It's a journey that continues, as there are always higher levels to reach for. As a wise person once said, "Life is a journey, not a destination." The key to happiness is to remember to enjoy the journey!

Seven Stepping Stones

I sincerely hope that the challenges you have faced do not rise to the level of the trauma of being caught in a SWAT team operation! Your life need not be a made-for-TV drama in order to feel the restless need for change or the desire to discover a passionate sense of purpose. Whatever challenges you face, whether large or small, you have the power to take charge and transform your life. It's easy to view yourself as a victim of circumstance and to take the path of least resistance. The status quo has its heels dug in deep. But with intention and conviction, you can become the master of your destiny and chart a path to a rich and robust life that will bring you joy, greater well-being, and a wonderful sense of satisfaction.

What I offer you in this book is a synthesis of all the tools, strategies, insights, and inspirations that I have gathered throughout my own personal journey and my professional training and experience as a life coach. I have distilled what I have learned into Seven Stepping Stones that will illuminate the path that will take you from where you are today to where you want to be.

Throughout the book you will find questions to ponder and suggestions for activities to pursue that are designed to assist you in moving forward through the stepping stone process. For your convenient reference, I have included a summary of questions and activities in a resource section at the back of the book.

I wish you joyful insights as you embark on your own journey of self-discovery and ultimately spread your wings to fly unabashedly into a future filled with exciting opportunity and freedom to create the quality of life that makes your heart sing! Together we will find the way to give wings to your dreams!

Part I:

Honoring Your Needs,
Desires, and Dreams

"And the day came, when the

risk to remain tight in a bud

was more painful than the

risk it took to blossom."

–Anaïs Nin

◆ Stepping Stone One:

Refueling Your Tank and Renewing Your Spirit

Shoring up your energy for change

> *"I am beginning to learn that it is the*
> *sweet simple things of life*
> *which are the real ones after all."*
>
> –Laura Ingalls Wilder

I have found that clients come to me most often when they are experiencing a career crisis, a relationship crisis, a spiritual crisis, or a health crisis. It's very rare to have a new client come to me who feels her life is working well and wants to make it even better! I do often have clients seek me out who are responding to a longing to embark on a new direction in life and are searching for greater meaning and a sense of purpose. I find, though, that most often the strongest desire for change follows a major life crisis or transition that has shaken our world and gotten our attention.

Perhaps you have just come through a painful divorce, have lost a coveted job, or have weathered a wrenching family crisis.

Perhaps the stresses of life and career challenges have left you feeling job burnout or even burnout on life in general. More often than not, major life events are thrust upon us catching us unprepared, without the mental, emotional, or physical resources to gracefully cope with a rainy day.

The idea of embarking on a new direction can seem compelling yet hopeless and heartless if we lack the energy to get started. What stops us from heeding the ever-increasing nudges we feel to move in a new direction? Plain and simple, it often boils down to two little words: "I'm tired."

Health and well-being are the first essential ingredients for embracing change. No matter how desperately you may desire something new for your life, and how strong the impulse to charge ahead with a quick fix, the first Stepping Stone on the path to giving wings to your dreams is to actually stand still! Take time for yourself and find ways to rest, relax, and rejuvenate. You've got to refuel your tank and renew your spirit in order to shore up your energy for change.

I am speaking from my heart on this issue and from the wellspring of personal experience. I had been strong and nurturing for my children throughout the drama of my ex-husband's drug ordeal, but I had completely neglected my own well-being. I was profoundly tired, feeling physically twenty years older, with a body that seemed on strike. Though I feared the repercussions and impact on my career, taking a medical leave of absence was a gift and a significant turning point in my life. It allowed me to stop the world and get off. It gave me the chance to regain my health and to see clearly what was truly important in my life and to make decisions that would propel me in a new and more satisfying direction.

Running on Empty

Fortunately, not every woman drives herself to the point of illness, creating no choice but to step out of the rat race for a little while. Yet without such a dramatic excuse, most people, particularly women, find it extremely difficult to shift perspective enough to create time and space to nurture themselves. I have noticed this is often true even for the most accomplished and outwardly powerful women.

Saddled with so many obligations, our innate desire to care for others and the prevailing belief that we should be able to do it all with grace and gusto, leaves so many of us running on empty. Probably the most damaging belief is the one that says we are supposed to put ourselves last—that a good woman is a selfless woman. This is so ingrained that we think nothing of running ourselves into the ground, and wearing a mental badge of honor as we do it. We do it so unconsciously that we never stop to notice the negative impact our selfless behavior has on our families.

Do our husbands want an exhausted, resentful wife? Do our children benefit from an unhappy, irritable mother? Do our friends delight in our being constantly on edge? It's a win-win situation when we put ourselves first. Why does the airline hostess implore us to put on our own air mask first in the case of emergency? Because we will be of little use to our children if we pass out from lack of oxygen!

It is absolutely essential as we contemplate moving in a new direction to take time for ourselves. It takes a lot of energy to change the status quo. Starting from a place of burnout and depleted energy can only lead to disappointment. The reason for our burnout is not just the misfit of our current job, the stress of dealing with difficult people, juggling too many responsibilities, or handling a personal crisis—at its core, our burnout is because we've continually put our needs last. It's time to put your own needs first! It's time to get quiet, and to put a priority on nurturing mind, body, and spirit.

For many, this advice seems counterintuitive. When I found myself on a medical leave of absence, precipitated in part by major job stress, my first instinct was to start working like crazy to hunt for a new job as I couldn't bear the thought of having to return to the same job. Years earlier, I had discovered a coach who specialized in helping women through life transitions. She helped me make a successful re-entry into the workforce after I chose to stay home with my kids for seven years. I trusted her implicitly.

I sought out the advice of this coach at the beginning of my medical leave and she advised me to do nothing about a new job search for at least the next thirty days. I thought, "You've got to be kidding me!" But it was hard to argue with the fact that I needed to follow doctor's orders to rest.

In Search of Joy

My coach advised that instead of embarking on a frenzied job search that I put a priority on choosing activities that would give me joy and nurture my body and soul. Joy? Finding joy seemed like an unnatural act and I really didn't even know where to begin the search. My feelings of joy had been so buried and seemed such a distant memory that I wasn't even sure I'd recognize the feeling if it surfaced! On top of that, I had been juggling the demands of my career and single motherhood for so long that any desires I might have had to do things just for fun had long since languished on the back burner.

Though it made obvious sense, I had a dreadful time giving myself permission to slow down and smell the roses. When you've been living non-stop in the fast lane, it can be really hard to know what to do with yourself when you find you've been given the luxury of time off with no obligations or commitments.

I had the support of a very wise doctor. Probably the single most helpful thing that he prescribed for me was a stress-reduction clinic that focused on mindfulness meditation. I had very little exposure to meditation and those few attempts had been aborted rather quickly and I felt a failure, as I wasn't ever able to get my mind to shut up! Either that, or I'd just fall asleep and miss the experience altogether.

This meditation class was different because it was held in a hospital and I found myself in the company of men and women who were also in the class for health reasons. The majority of the class attendees were in desperate circumstances. These folks were fighting for their lives to overcome the ravages of cancer, or living with debilitating chronic pain. For some this class was their last hope to elude a terminal diagnosis. My health issues seemed so minor by comparison. My eyes had been opened to the reality that life is indeed short, and quality of life was to be cherished. I made a firm commitment to stick with the program.

As a result, I learned the skill of being mindful. It was a new experience for me to just get quiet, go inside, and focus on the joy of the present moment. I gained a new appreciation and gratitude for the little pleasures in life, like watching my youngest son belt out a triple on the baseball field! I realized how pathetic I had been, going to his baseball games and tapping my foot impatiently, wondering when his game would ever end so I could get back to all the things I had to do.

One day I had this incredible experience of just being in the moment at one of his games and drinking in the beauty that surrounded me—the vibrant green of the hills, the billowing clouds overhead, the budding cherry blossoms, the cool breeze in my hair. I noticed the laughter of the boys and the exuberance with which they played. And I felt pure joy in that moment. It changed my experience of little league baseball and life itself. From that moment on, I looked forward to the games and I immersed myself in the experience of being where I was, not ten other places in my mind. And I experienced a sense of inner peace that had eluded me and I felt stirrings of my energy beginning to return.

I began to follow my coach's advice and seek activities that would be joyful and fun for me. Years earlier, a co-worker had taken a sabbatical and had come back enthused about the Artist's Way workshop she had attended. She was totally jazzed and excited about the song lyrics she had begun to write as a result of removing the blocks to her creativity. I had filed that away as an intriguing idea, something I'd like to do...someday.

My someday had arrived, it seemed, as I had time and the marching orders to go find something fun to do! So I tried searching on the Internet for a class but wasn't able to find one. Discouraged, I went on an outing to one of my favorite bookstores. I thought I could at least buy the book. As I reached to open the door at the East West Bookshop, I stopped in my tracks. There was a poster in the window advertising an Artist's Way workshop, starting that very week! As the saying goes, when the student is ready, the teacher appears.

The Artist's Way is a book written by Julia Cameron that offers a 12-week program for releasing blocks to creative expression. One of the things she passionately recommends is the practice of writing what she calls the Morning Pages. Morning Pages are the daily practice of creating three hand-written journal pages first thing in the morning, every morning. It is an amazing thing. It starts out like a brain dump and very often a place to vent all the negative, angry, hurt, and otherwise awful feelings we have bottled up inside. But pretty soon, an amazing thing happens. The complaining, the whining, and the mundane scribbles give way to the birthing of new ideas, exciting thoughts of possibilities, and the joy of creative expression.

After about three weeks, I was astonished when my daily pages became beautiful expressions of heartfelt poetry that reached deep inside me to a place that had been locked up and longing for release. I was delighted. The last time I had written a poem had been when I was seven years old. I won first prize in a poetry contest, an achievement I had completely forgotten. It was therapeutic to say the least, allowing myself free rein to speak my heart, express my truth, and access parts of me that had all but atrophied. I had found my joy in creative expression!

Extreme Self-Care

You don't need to take a sabbatical or get sick and take a medical leave of absence to take the time to nurture yourself and embark on joyful pursuits. It's a pathetic statement of how we've been conditioned to de-value our personal needs as women to think that it requires an extreme circumstance to be able to find the time to have a little self-affirming fun and to nurture ourselves.

In the life coaching profession, a term has emerged that captures the essence of the importance of self-nurturing. It's called "extreme self-care." I was a guest on a radio show discussing this topic and my host was joking about the concept being so foreign: "Is that a soda? Is that a sport? I can't even get to self-care, let alone extreme self-care!"

The fact that extreme self-care has emerged as a concept speaks to the fact that in our society we tend to deny ourselves the basics of loving kindness. In order to create a new habit, sometimes you have to overshoot the desired behavior to jumpstart a new reality. We have to get out of the habit of neglecting our very real needs, of neglecting those activities that give us quality of life, of neglecting those things that ultimately allow us to be more present to those around us. In order to get out of the deeply entrenched habit of self-neglect, we must turn our attention to extreme self-care.

As women, we know all about nurturing. We pride ourselves on the care we lavish on our loved ones, but most of us simply do not know how to lavish that same care on ourselves. We feel selfish. I speak frequently to audiences of women in all professions and all levels of income. Without exception, the overriding reaction to the idea that we deserve to take time for ourselves is one of trepidation. "People will think I'm selfish," or more to the point, "That feels selfish."

It is not selfish to care for yourself. Everyone around you benefits when you feel good, energetic, inspired, and joyful. You have so much more to give others when you regularly take time for yourself. When you refuse to allow yourself the pursuit of simple pleasures and time for nurturing self-care, it may seem of no consequence in the moment, but over time, burnout is the inevitable outcome. When you reach a state of burnout, you really have no choice but to embark on a course of extreme self-care, unless you are prepared to stay stuck in the misery of lethargy.

Extreme self-care is a mechanism to give yourself permission to take time for yourself and to break out of the paradigm, the belief system that says, "It's not okay to take care of myself." It's about getting back to the core of understanding what really feeds you, what's important to you, what your body and soul needs to feel whole again. Extreme self-care gives you the focus to do that. Get a massage, have a spa day, spend an afternoon on the beach or on a blanket in a park, get out your watercolors, sleep in late on the weekends, go on a road trip, book a vacation.

Place a priority on doing things solely for your own pleasure, for your healing, for your well-being. Cut yourself some slack. Let some balls drop if you must. Say "No" more often to make time for you. Avoid making life-changing decisions or pushing yourself in a new direction until you have given yourself a chance to refuel your tank and renew your spirit. You'll make far better decisions and feel re-energized to take productive action.

Nearly every woman I've ever coached in my practice has been challenged in some way by this concept. In fact, some are so challenged by the idea that they will abandon our coaching relationship and either look for a kick-butt coach who will push them into action in spite of their fatigue or they'll forget about the journey altogether. Sure, you can push ahead when you are maxed out physically and emotionally...for a while. I have been there and done that. My observation is that those who neglect their very real need to care for themselves will eventually succumb to a serious health issue, some for which there is no recovery.

Let's face it. When we are tired, we aren't being very productive anyway, so what's to stop us from taking a little time off? Think about it as an investment. Whether an hour a day, an afternoon a week, a week's vacation, or a three-month sabbatical, the time off you take right now will pay dividends in higher productivity tomorrow. More important, it will build a stronger foundation of health and well-being to support you as you begin moving along the path to give wings to your dreams.

Janice began working with me when she had reached the end of her rope at work. She was feeling a desperate need to change careers. She had worked herself into a physical and emotional basket case by giving it all at the office. In her case, the office was the emergency room of the local hospital. She was a very skilled trauma nurse. The problem was, the hospital was understaffed and what little staff they had was lacking proper experience. Janice felt everything fell on her shoulders and in her case she was literally dealing with life or death situations. She routinely worked 16-hour days on her feet, taking on extra shifts to fill in any time she was asked. She felt no power to say no. She had set no boundaries. She had become crabby and resentful. In her words, she'd become a "snarling hornet of negativity." She wasn't sleeping at night, tossing and turning, worrying about situations at work and worrying about what people thought of her. She felt her best efforts were not good enough. She felt defeated, angry, and powerless to change her situation at work. She believed the only way to get relief was to leave. She was desperate for time to herself but felt too much guilt and responsibility to even ask for it.

Janice wanted a new job and she wanted it now. I subscribe to the belief that "wherever you go, there you are." Though I felt I could assist her in finding a new job, it was clear to me she'd be showing up exhausted, unhappy, and likely to repeat her pattern of giving it all at the office. I encouraged Janice to slow down just a bit and take a closer look at what she really needed. And what she needed were some real basics of self-care. She was not eating well, she was not sleeping well, she wasn't exercising, and she was not doing anything to relax or play. She literally did not have the time.

The first thing we did together was to brainstorm ways she could make more time. The first was that she simply had to start saying "No" more often. But before she could even conceive of doing that, we had to address her issue of self-worth. Like many women, she had tied her self-esteem to feeling needed by others and therefore giving others whatever they asked for. She had given everything she had to the point of utter mental, physical, and emotional exhaustion. We established that she was indeed valued by the hospital and that they truly needed her and appreciated her. She began to see that she had limited her options to an all-or-nothing scenario and that it would truly be a win-win for her and the hospital to negotiate a schedule that would prevent her from quitting and would give Janice back an opportunity to have a life! Additionally, Janice began to see that even though she could do a job quicker and better by herself, she was enabling the other nurses to stay inexperienced and dependent on her. She began to make a point to assist the other nurses and train them so that they could become more self-sufficient. She started saying "No" to extra shifts, forcing the hospital to find other resources. She carved out enough time to take quiet time for herself each morning and each evening for meditation, for exercise, for spiritual reading, for preparing healthy meals, for taking long hot baths. She started with committing to this only two times a week, then gradually increased until she was taking daily time for herself. As she got better at establishing her boundaries and taking time for herself, she began to have time for friends again and even started dating. And within a couple of months, an amazing thing happened. She realized she was no longer miserable at work. She had built a life and she was showing up relaxed, rested, and happy at work. People were saying "Who are you and what have you done with Janice?!"

Self-care covers a lot of territory. Taking care of physical and emotional well-being is obvious to most, but there are other categories to consider. Depending on who you are, you might also want to put emphasis on activities that are mentally stimulating or those that excite your creative juices. For many, creating a deeper spiritual connection and commitment to spiritual practice is key to getting grounded and back to center. Finally, I recommend attention to enhancing your surroundings to create a space for yourself that is calm, orderly, and nurturing. Let's look at the challenges and opportunities to nurture ourselves in each of these important aspects of life.

Go Out and Play!

We live in a society that implores us to "work until the work is done." But is the work really ever done? Whether you are a housewife or a software engineer, guilt seems to dictate a reality of all work and no play. This very pervasive belief system is what creates a culture that rewards workaholics, leaving a trail of destruction in the form of burnout and profound fatigue. So many people wake up one day in mid-life realizing they've given it all at the office or to the management of a household that they have lost the most precious things in life—they've lost track of their most important values. Relationships crumble, kids suffer neglect, and activities that used to bring joy are a thing of the past. We've lost sight of the importance of play!

I encourage you to find ways to bring a spirit of playfulness into your life. Remember the things you used to love to do when life was simpler and you didn't have so many obligations? Bring those activities back into your life! Spend time doing things that are fun, joyful, and stimulating to you. Carve out time for play. Schedule time for fun on your calendar. Schedule fun? We all think fun is supposed to be spontaneous. But in our busy and burdened lives, if we wait for spontaneous opportunities to have fun, we'll be waiting a very long time.

If you love the outdoors, work in the garden, get out and go for a walk in a scenic place, go for a hike, go boating, go surfing, go camping, pack a picnic and go to the park or out to the country-side. If you are someone who thrives on mental stimulation, read some books, go to lectures, join a discussion group on a topic that interests you. If you are someone who thrives on creative expression, go to museums, places in nature, places with good people watching, get out your journals, your canvas, your clay, or whatever supports your brand of creative expression.

Do you have a longing to create something artistic but have no recognizable skill? Sign up for a class in something that interests you. Allow yourself to be bad at it! Do it for fun, for the process of learning to do something new; don't compare yourself to Picasso or even the student next to you. Do it for the joy of it, and don't judge your creation! Pretend you are five years old again and know it takes time and it takes practice to excel. I'm sure some artists are born, but most are products of desire and training and perseverance.

Do you have hobbies that have languished from lack of attention? Dig out your tools, your supplies, and your commitment to get started again. Have your hobbies fallen victim to a lack of space? Clear out a corner of a room or the garage and make the space for you to play. Spending time on activities that we love gives us such a boost of positive energy. It's a great stress reducer and a great way to refuel your tank. People who take time to play on a regular basis have more satisfying and joyful lives.

Taking Care of Your Physical Body

I have struggled with a variety of physical health issues for as long as I can remember. I had asthma as a child. I grew out of that, only to be plagued with chronic and persistent food and environmental allergies. I discovered I had a low-thyroid problem and have struggled with anemia, low blood sugar, and hormone imbalances, including adrenal exhaustion. One thing I know about is fatigue.

I have been a seeker of magic elixirs to feel physically better my whole life. I have availed myself of all manner of doctors and alternative health providers like chiropractors and acupuncturists, even tiptoeing into the realm of energy healers and psychics from time to time. I have seen my share of therapists as well. I've had my nose in countless books searching for cures. I am totally open to alternative approaches to health management, because when fatigue is the major complaint, it can be very complicated to get to the bottom of it.

If you are suffering from fatigue or any of the multitudes of stress-related illnesses, please seek the assistance of one or more health professionals to get a full check-up and lab workup to see if there is a physical basis for your fatigue that can be medically treated. If your tests are all fine that doesn't mean it's all in your head! You may be nutritionally depleted or emotionally burdened. Do check into nutrition advisors or other alternative health providers who might offer a course of treatment not available from traditional sources.

I also recommend the services of a good therapist to get at the source of any emotional issues that may be contributing to your stress symptoms. Profound fatigue can be a sign of depression. Depression can be treated in a variety of ways—if you suspect you are suffering from depression, please do not hesitate to ask for help. If you are sick and tired of being sick and tired, get the help you need to support your body in healing both physically and emotionally.

Symptoms of fatigue are exacerbated by being overweight. Struggling with weight gain has been another familiar companion of mine. Eating for stress, eating to console myself, and eating to hide from emotional truths had been a way of life for me. One needed only to look at my physique to judge my state of contentment with life or lack thereof. Needless to say, in times of emotional turmoil, I put on a lot of extra weight. Learning to take care of my body has been vital to my well-being.

After all is said and done, and after all the searching for magic elixirs, it really does boil down to a willingness and a commitment to doing the things we all know are necessary to bring our bodies to optimum health and well-being: exercise and eat right. And I think most of us find that is not easy. With a combination of traditional and alternative medical assistance, nutritional support, emotional housecleaning, and a newfound commitment to self-care, I found my way to the healthiest body and the highest energy levels I have ever had.

Years ago I ran across an affirmation in a book that really stuck with me. "My body is the temple of my soul." I absolutely loved this statement. It is a wonderful thought to keep front and center because the tendency to self-loathing (as in "I hate my body") is so great when you are overweight. Thinking of your body as the temple of your soul opens the door to greater self-love and self-care so that your body receives the nurturing and commitment to action that will support healthy well-being.

One thing I learned for myself about being overweight is that it is vital to love and accept yourself exactly the way you are before you can be successful creating the body you really want. Self-loathing and harsh judgment feeds on itself and creates a vicious cycle of punishing and counter-productive behaviors.

Dress yourself well even if you are overweight. Buy yourself a few things to wear that support you in feeling beautiful now. You can always get them altered later. Do your nails. Invest in quality hair care and makeup. Treat yourself as the beautiful woman that you are, one who is learning to make healthier choices for her body.

If you embark on a weight loss program, do it for your health and approach it as a loving, nurturing thing to do for your body. Enjoy the process as your body responds in ways that make you proud in the mirror as well. Think in terms of self-nurturing choices rather than deprivation.

Impatience and the expectation that we should implement our new habits perfectly are the enemies of permanent weight loss. It took years of old habits to get us where we are today. Allow yourself time and be gentle with yourself for temporary lapses. Accept that the best way to get where you want to be is a slow but steady commitment rather than the quick-fix diet du jour.

And don't forget to drink water! A lot of women, myself included, tend to eat when we are really thirsty. I've been told over and over, particularly by alternative, natural health professionals, that drinking a lot of water is the most overlooked healthful and healing habit. We spend fortunes on supplements and diet assistance and forget to do the one thing that costs very little and is so basic to high functioning bodies and optimal well-being. Drink water!

Taking Care of Yourself Emotionally

Some of the most satisfying parts of my journey have come from learning to pay attention to my emotional needs and well-being and finding ways to release old triggers and old patterns that no longer serve me. When life hasn't turned out quite the way you expected, you may find yourself wracked with regrets and disappointment. It's easy to get caught up in beating yourself up for past choices and current circumstances. I have found it most helpful to remember this truth: We always do the best we can, given our belief systems, our level of knowledge, and our experience at the time. No one makes a deliberate choice that would put them in harm's way or end in disaster. The key is to recognize the past is in the past! Given the same set of circumstances today, we would apply our newfound knowledge, experiences, and updated beliefs to make a different decision.

Sometimes we become conscious that we have a pattern of getting in similar unhealthy situations over and over again. That feeds our inner critic to feel justified in bashing us for our stupidity. If you look at it closely, you'll realize that hindsight really is 20/20. At the time, to our conscious minds, the situation must have been disguised in some way, preventing us from seeing what was clearly a pattern in retrospect.

It is important to clear away emotional baggage to make way for new and healthier choices. We tend to make decisions about ourselves based on past experiences that can be very limiting. In order to move forward to create a new and satisfying reality, we must learn to be gentle and compassionate with ourselves. Learn to forgive yourself and others for being less than perfect human beings.

Getting stuck in the negative energy of anger, blame, and resentment is like putting the old Berlin Wall between you and happiness. And like the Berlin Wall itself, with the right tools and the right attitude, old negative patterns can indeed crumble away. A friend of mine once said, "Resentment is like swallowing poison and expecting someone else to die." Resolve to move forward with a positive inner energy.

Easier said than done, you might be thinking! There are a myriad of self-help books and workshops available to help you conquer old patterns and release emotional pain that serves to keep you stuck. I have found in my life that just the right book or just the right workshop opportunity will cross my path at just the right time. I have learned to trust my intuition and go with whatever I find intriguing in the moment. If I find I have gotten in over my head emotionally, I will set up some time with a therapist to work through the difficult issue.

Depending on your level of need and/or resistance, you may want to seek the services of a licensed therapist to support your emotional healing process. Just as in the medical field, there are traditional and non-traditional approaches to therapy. I have found working with a therapist who practices a technique called EMDR (Eye Movement Desensitization and Reprocessing) to be really helpful in getting to the source of an issue by allowing access to your subconscious to locate where a trauma or a painful association is stored and to consciously release this old, stuck energy. This technique along with traditional talk therapy seems to really speed up the process of healing so that you can move on more quickly.

Throughout this book, I will share with you a number of tools, techniques, and strategies designed to support your emotional well-being. If you find yourself confronted or upset by the process of self-exploration, please do seek the assistance of a therapist to support you in blasting through the emotional blocks that may be holding you back, keeping you stuck in the past, and unable to create a new reality that is fulfilling and inspiring.

Conquering Chaos

All we have talked about so far are ways to shore up your energy for change, to create a foundation of strength and positive energy from which to launch yourself productively on the journey toward new endeavors. One of the common issues that gets in the way of moving forward and that tends to drain our energy is living in a state of mental and physical clutter and chaos.

It's important to clear the decks of unfinished business and to create a reasonable sense of order in our lives to create the mental energy for our new ventures. Do you have a laundry list of unfinished business that haunts you? Making a list of outstanding commitments, projects, and obligations is a place to start. Then with the precision of a surgeon, take a mental scalpel to the list. What really must be done? And must it be done by you? Can you delegate to a family member or friend? Can you hire professional help? Of the things on your list, is there anything that could justifiably be postponed to a later date without impacting you—as in a "nice-to-do" rather than a "must-do"? Of the things remaining, what one item on this list would free up the greatest amount of your energy if the task were complete? Commit to finding a way to finish this task at your earliest opportunity, preferably by asking for appropriate help. It's amazing how much unfinished business contributes to our fatigue and how much positive energy you'll feel when it's no longer hanging over your head.

For many people the state of their physical environment has a direct impact on their level of productive energy. Is your environment nurturing and aesthetically pleasing to you? Does it reflect your personality, does it contain art or other decorations that please you. Is it orderly enough that it serves your needs well? Or are you living in a constant state of chaos and clutter? For now, I would recommend taking some steps to create an environment that is visually pleasing to you, free of obvious clutter and disorder. Hire some help—professional organizers are a gift from God as far as I'm concerned because I simply do not have the wherewithal to create and maintain order where paperwork is concerned!

Taking Care of Yourself Spiritually

My final recommendation for shoring up your energy for change is to encourage you to make time to honor your personal spiritual beliefs. If you practice a religion, recommit to the activities that feed you spiritually. If you do not practice a religion, but consider yourself spiritual, do the things that give you that feeling of wonder and connection with the divine.

If you don't think of yourself as spiritual in any way, I would invite you to at least explore the power of getting quiet in some way. Try basic meditations such as focusing on your breath to quiet your mind and just allow yourself to get in touch with your deepest self. Activities like yoga are healthy for the body and meditative as well. Many day-to-day activities, if done mindfully with deliberate intention, can create a deep sense of relaxation and spiritual well-being: working in the garden, writing in a journal, walking with focus on experiencing your surroundings, swimming laps in a pool, or rhythmic jogging.

Taking time for yourself to refuel your tank and renew your spirit is a critical stepping stone on the journey to give wings to your dreams. When you begin to spread your wings to fly, you'll want to have the strength and stamina to go the distance. As I have learned for myself, patience is indeed a virtue. I'm fond of saying, "Slow down, you'll get there faster!" And what I mean by "there" is the place you truly desire to go. You can accomplish so much by getting quiet, by changing pace, by allowing yourself to play, and by nurturing your body, mind and spirit. It is precious indeed to have abundant energy to follow your dreams.

Getting In Touch With Your Deepest Desires

Resurrecting the dreams you left behind

"When sleeping women wake, mountains move."

–Chinese Proverb

When I was a little girl, I remember being spellbound as I watched a motivational speaker on PBS. I remember feeling a giddy excitement as his words of inspiration came through the television set and enveloped my heart and soul. I knew at that moment that I wanted to be like him when I grew up. I wanted to reach out to people with a message of hope and possibility and to make people happy.

Looking back, I had so much clarity at a young age as to who I was and what I was about. Yet that clarity got lost in the shuffle of growing up and conforming to the expectations of those around me. The practical side of me and the chorus of grownups in my life all convinced me that a career in computers was where it was at.

I had other dreams, of course. I wanted to study clinical psychology, recognizing my deep desire to help people improve the quality of their lives. I have always been highly empathetic and I became convinced, and probably rightly so, by people who loved me, that I'd become a basket case taking on everyone else's pain! I wanted to be a journalist, recognizing my gift with words and feeling drawn to giving expression to my creativity. "No, you don't want to do that," my father said, "Journalists work for peanuts." Then I thought I'd be a landscape architect, combining my creativity, love of color, beauty, and nature (but then I did have to consider my pollen allergies!) By my senior year in high school, I had settled on my desire to be a fashion designer, but that was considered too much of a long shot and definitely not practical. Besides, the fashion college was out of town and costly. My parents were not on board for that. My father was convinced the future was in computers and accounting. So, I opted to commute to the University of Houston and study business and computer technology.

I had dreams, passions, and creative energy that, with all good intention, became stifled and stuffed away in a long-forgotten place. I can tell you that computers bored me to tears. I struggled for years to make myself read the trade journals in the computer industry. So often I would catch myself re-reading the same sentence over and over again—I just didn't really care!

I would have thought I had some kind of reading disability except for the fact that when I was reading something I was interested in, this was never a problem. When reading a personal growth book on a topic that was a current issue in my life, I couldn't put it down. I absorbed books like these easily and effortlessly. Over the years I began to think there was a message in that. What if I could be in a line of work where I loved the required reading! What if I could find a way to make a career out of my personal passion? That was a quiet longing of mine that remained dormant for two decades.

Throughout those years, I found myself drawn again and again to personal growth seminars. Inevitably, I would fantasize being the one in the front of the room inspiring people to embrace positive change. I longed to be in a line of work that made a difference in the world, that had a positive impact on people rather than simply contributing to a corporate bottom line. The little girl in me was relentlessly jumping up and down, trying to get my attention to no avail. My programming was deeply ingrained: "Oh, you are just a dreamer! Let's get back to being practical."

Just a Dreamer

As children and young adults we are often judged or ridiculed for being dreamers. Yet, it is our dreams that create energy, passion, and zest for life. Abandoned dreams create such sorrow, longing, and repression. The little child within is so tender and so impressionable. We take it to heart when those we depend on chastise us or tell us our dreams are not possible. We're told, "You can't do this…you can't do that…you should do this…you should do that"—and we buy it. Some of us were more fortunate in that we had a cheerleader telling us we could do anything we wanted; but more often than not, we were simultaneously discouraged from wanting anything too outlandish, and admonished to be practical about what it was we wanted!

No doubt the naysayers meant well. Perhaps they only wanted to protect us from the possibility of being disappointed. Perhaps they experienced the disappointment of their own shattered dreams and truly believed it's just not possible to have what we want. It is never too late to reclaim your dreams and listen to the call of your inner longings. The problem is that for many of us, those longings have become so deeply buried and barricaded from our conscious mind that we feel at a total loss to identify them. Some would say, "Sure, I'd like to give wings to my dreams…if only I knew what my dreams were!" The event of a mid-life crisis is often the catalyst that reawakens us to those longings and neglected dreams.

The beauty of the mid-life crisis so many of us experience, is that when all is said and done, we find a window has opened for us to explore what is missing in our lives. We find ourselves face to face with what we've left behind and find the motivation to reclaim our true selves. The longings come rushing back to the surface and will not be ignored.

Maybe you've reached mid-life without the crisis, but still have a nagging and persistent feeling that something is missing, that there is something more for you in life, that there is something you are meant to do.

Sometimes the search for meaning follows on the heels of a serious illness or injury that gets our attention, or the shock of the untimely loss of a loved one. That's when we face the reality that life is short and we no longer take our time here on Earth for granted. We find ourselves with an urgent and irrepressible urge to find more meaning in our lives. We want to find our sense of purpose, to make a lasting contribution…to leave a loving legacy.

Enjoy Life! This is Not a Dress Rehearsal!

Several years ago, I lost a dear friend and cherished mentor to brain cancer. Roseanne was a major go-getter of a woman, always at the top of her game and a loving mother of three exceptional children. She had inexplicably been laid off from her sales job that summer. It was astonishing because she was one of their top producers. She wasn't worried; she knew she could easily get another job; she only needed to decide what she wanted to do next. So I called her up one day and said, "Hey, Roseanne, have you got that new job yet?" There was a quiet sob on the phone. "What is it?" I asked gently. "I've just had surgery for a brain tumor," she said through her tears. "You are kidding me," I gasped. "No. I was having bad headaches for a couple of days and they became unbearable. I went to the emergency room on Friday and they operated on Saturday. Lauren, I am so scared," she sobbed. Oh my God. Roseanne was forty-nine years old. Six months later she was dead. Most of us aren't prepared for a life cut so dramatically short.

A few years later, I lost yet another friend to cancer. I met Deborah at a women's networking club shortly after moving to Santa Barbara. When I stood up during my first visit to the club and said I was in the business of helping women find their passion and purpose in life, I noticed one woman in particular seemed riveted on what I was saying. After I sat down, Deborah passed me a note saying, "I want to find my passion, can you help me?"

Soon after, we met for our first session together. She had built a successful career in corporate computer sales; however, she had just experienced her second layoff in fifteen months and was seriously burned out on the idea of returning to a similar job. She was forty-nine years old and wanted to take her career in a new, more personally satisfying direction. I asked her if she had any ideas and she said, "Oh yes, I would love to be in real estate sales!" After just a few sessions together, Deborah determined that being in real estate wasn't just an idle dream, it was in fact what she deeply desired and together we created a plan for her to take the necessary steps to get there.

To this day I believe Deborah had an angel on her shoulder. Everything fell into place so smoothly that in less than six months she had passed the real estate exam, found a broker to hire and mentor her, and sold not one, but two houses! She was the talk of the agency! A few months later, Deborah held a huge fiftieth birthday celebration that I attended. She stood before the crowd just glowing and exuberant about the quality of life she had attained for herself. I will never forget the electricity in the air as she expressed her gratitude and set herself up as an example that dreams do indeed come true.

Less than a year later, Deborah was diagnosed with lung cancer, a disease with very dismal statistics for survival. But Deborah had spirit and determination and a positive attitude. She became somewhat of a poster child for fighting cancer as she beat the odds and was pronounced cancer-free. With such gratitude in her heart, Deborah decided to live life to the fullest, paying attention to acting on desires and dreams she had yet to fulfill. She took a trip to Europe featuring a visit to Wimbledon, the ultimate expression of her love for tennis. She got the facelift she'd been longing for. She bought the clothes and the furniture that made her heart sing. She made a choice to live life to the fullest as she had learned life is precious, and all you can really count on is today.

It broke the hearts of all who knew her, including the medical team that had been in such awe of her spirit, when the diagnosis turned out to be incorrect. A few months down the road, she learned her cancer had metastasized into her brain and was inoperable. Deborah was faced with a truly terminal diagnosis. Friends swarmed around her and cared for her until the end. Deborah died peacefully in her home, in the arms of a dear friend at the age of fifty-two.

The only time we are guaranteed is right now. I have one of those pin-on buttons that says "Enjoy life! This is not a dress rehearsal." This is so true! If the life you are living is not bringing you joy, it's time to make some changes. But first, you've got to really get to know yourself, to get connected to what's really important for your quality of life. And yes, to revisit those childhood dreams. Ask yourself what you truly value in life and take a look to see if the life you are living matches up to your list. Living a life incongruent with our deepest-held values leads to chronic lack of joy and fulfillment, to apathy and burnout.

Life gets complicated. Somewhere along the way most of us lose track of what's really important to us. A series of misadventures or disappointments may have us disillusioned as well. Circumstances may seem to present a case that we have lost any choice in what happens to us. Dreams can seem very elusive if not downright frivolous.

I have had the opportunity to work with young women— seniors in high school and college girls—and I have found the experience very personally fulfilling. I remember the first time I worked with a young girl, I saw myself in her. She had high ideals, was smart, had a good head on her shoulders, and knew what she wanted in life. At the same time, I saw red flags shooting out all over the place when she would start to talk about boyfriends. Still in this day and age of feminine empowerment, young women are so ready to sacrifice all in the name of love.

I am passionate about supporting young women to get firmly grounded in who they are and what they truly want in life and to be very, very conscious about the relationships they enter, such that the partner they choose in life is one who will be the hoist for her sails and not the anchor around her ankles. My hope for young women today is that they always remember who they are so that they avoiding finding themselves lost in midlife searching to find their way back to themselves!

At age forty-two I found myself utterly lost and confused, my sense of identity shattered, my picture of what life was supposed to look like totally debunked. Like the proverbial rug had been yanked out from under me. My only recognizable dream in the moment was for a life free of drama and trauma. Yet deep inside I had vague yearnings and a growing need to pay attention to the little girl in me who was screaming for acknowledgement.

I returned to the pursuits that gave me comfort, reading self-help books and enrolling in personal growth programs. I remember going to a workshop to explore what I loved, what I wished for. I realized that I had completely lost touch with who I was and what I wanted at the deepest level. My life had all the trappings of success up to the point where it all began to unravel. But I had never been truly happy. I felt no passion for my career of 15 years; it seemed only a powerful siphon that continually drained my energy. Until I found a career I was truly passionate about, burnout and lethargy remained my constant state. And I'm here to tell you, that's no way to live!

Finding Your Passion

It is very easy and quite common to jump from the frying pan into the fire when we find that a particular job, relationship, or other life circumstance is no longer working for us. It's easy to talk ourselves into believing we have no choices when we feel a great urgency to do something, anything to escape the discomfort. Sometimes just making the decision to seek a change and creating an intention to find something better will give us enough of an energy boost to be able to tolerate our current situation long enough to get our ducks lined up so that we can make an intelligent choice.

If you find yourself in a situation where you are in survival mode, of course you will have to make short-term decisions that may be considerably less than ideal. Do whatever you must in the moment to keep your head above water, but know that with time, attention, and intention, you can navigate yourself into a position to create what you really want.

For example, when a career decision is looming, very often, it's not a job change that is needed, it's a complete rethinking of the direction we want to go in life. Many of us have found ourselves moving along a career path that provided opportunity and income rewards without much deliberate planning or conscious choice on our part. Perhaps we started on the path to please a parent or at the urging of a friend. Maybe we weren't all that sure what we wanted to do and let the career path choose us by taking the first job we were offered and just went with the program from there. Then one day we wake up unhappy, burned out and feeling trapped in a line of work that has taken on a life of its own. Very often this job burnout is coupled with feeling trapped in a relationship that is no longer working for us, feeling we have lost touch with family and cherished friends, feeling disconnected from anything that feels like fun and on top of that we might even be angry at ourselves for the shape our body is in. Basically, it feels like nothing is working in our lives.

In this place of burnout or recovery from personal disaster everything seems bleak. We may have faint memories of how it felt to be alive with passion and energy once upon a time. The secret to regaining your passion for life is to reconnect with the desires, the dreams, the longings, and the passions you once held when you were younger and life was simpler. It's important to find a way to bring aspects of this forgotten part of you back into your life.

What Do You Really Love?

Think back to when you were a little girl. Roll back the hands of time until you connect with images of a time when you felt exuberance for life, a sense of joy and wonder, an unbridled happiness. What were you doing? Were your hands immersed in something tactile like finger paints or making mud pies? Were you engaged in a game of "let's pretend"? Were you climbing a tree? Riding a horse? Caressing a pet? Were you gazing at clouds and seeing pictures and intricate designs? Were you reading a book? Playing solitaire? Engaging in vivid imaginary adventures? Were you doing cartwheels in the grass? Jumping on a trampoline? Were you drawing pictures? Selecting the perfect crayon to adorn your favorite coloring book? Making silly faces? Making people laugh? Dancing in a tutu? Whatever memory comes up for you, immerse yourself in remembering the feeling. We are hunting for those memories that made us feel joyful, peaceful, safe, comforted, excited, happy, and content. This may seem silly or frivolous at first glance, but trust me, it is not. There are so many clues to be found in our childhood memories to help us better understand what makes us tick. To the extent possible, I would like you to identify at least one or two childhood loves and bring that experience into your life now.

Now, you might feel silly at your age climbing a tree (and it might not even be physically possible!) That doesn't mean you can't recreate the feeling experience you had when climbing a tree. Ask yourself what was it about climbing trees that exhilarated you? Was it the physical act of climbing? Was it the thrill of being high above the ground and discovering new vistas? Was it the feeling of being all alone in your own world for a little while where no one could intrude on your thoughts?

If you are willing and able, by all means, go find a tree and climb it! If you are not, then identify the attributes of the experience and think about what other activities might give you the same level of satisfaction. Perhaps hiking or driving to a vista point and spending time contemplating life from a new perspective would recreate that special feeling. You get the idea. Look for creative ways to feed your soul and renew your spirit, taking your cues from memories of activities that used to make you feel so good inside. It's a first step toward reawakening your passions. It's a gift that probably won't even cost much, but that will make your heart sing and your energy soar. It's a fun and effective way to get reacquainted with you!

Lori grew up in a landlocked state, but even as a child she was passionate about the ocean and all its creatures. Her bedroom featured blue paint with pictures of dolphins swimming all around. She loved animals of all kinds and she was always drawing pictures of them. When she was nine years old, she was given her first camera and she loved taking pictures of all the neighborhood pets. She thought she'd like to be a veterinarian when she grew up until she realized that entailed cutting into animals and sewing them up! She loved to draw, so she modified her aspirations and decided she wanted to be an animal artist. Somewhere along the line, she decided that she wasn't very good at drawing and put that dream to rest in the recesses of her mind, but she never stopped taking photographs of animals.

Lori's first career was as a vocational rehabilitation counselor, working with the physically, mentally, and emotionally disabled. After several years she followed an urge to work in the outdoors and became a firefighter in a seaside town. After a few years of living by the ocean she decided to go back to school to study marine science. This path took her on a long and impressive list of oceanic adventures in Hawaii, Alaska, Europe and the South Pacific, where she always had her camera along and spent her spare time capturing the beauty of nature's magnificent creatures. She sold a few photographs here and there and even had a photo published in *National Geographic* magazine—every photographer's dream! But mostly her boxes and boxes of photos remained tucked away in her closet.

After eight years of thinking about it, Lori decided to re-energize her childhood dream and put herself out in the world as an artist. We worked together to help her clarify her vision and to overcome obstacles. Recently, she launched her beautiful marine wildlife photography website showcasing her stunning images.

The power of our childhood dreams cannot be ignored. It's just amazing the wisdom we carry at such a young age and how deeply we can bury the knowledge of our gifts and our calling! I see it again and again—the longings of our childhood often come to the forefront in midlife to give us another opportunity to recognize and act on the passions that will bring us the greatest happiness and satisfaction with our lives

If you don't remember much about being a really small child, that's okay, just fast forward to a time you do remember and go through the same process. Try starting at five years old, then ten years old, then fifteen, and then twenty. You can keep going for as long as you like. The objective is to discover things you have loved that you may have for one reason or another abandoned—perhaps in the name of being responsible, of being a hard worker, of being just slammed with too much to do, not enough time or not enough money. Maybe you've experienced a slow, steady but pervasive shift away from paying attention to what is important to you, in order to meet the needs and obligations imposed by others: work associates, family, social circle, spiritual community. Seek and find the activities and experiences you've left behind. If you want to experience more enjoyment in life and career, it's important to bring elements of what you love into the picture, whether your career revolves around them or they feed you so that you are more energized for the work you do in the world. For example, many artistic, highly creative people may find that making a career out of their art takes the joy out of it, as they may not enjoy the realities of sales, marketing, and administering a business. It is essential for these folks to make time for artistic/creative expression as a hobby or to take periodic retreats to immerse themselves in the joy of it. This keeps them balanced and energetic, which feeds their emotional and physical well-being.

What Do You Deeply Value?

Another way of getting reacquainted with dreams and longings left behind is to get really clear about your personal values. When I say "values" I'm not only talking about "family values" and things like trust, honesty, ethics, and love. I'm also talking about the things you value in terms of the experience you desire to have in your life. Do you value a sense of achievement, adventure, or autonomy? Do you value compassion, connection, or contribution? Do you value happiness, health, or humor? Do you value influence, independence, or integrity? Do you value personal growth, partnership, or privacy? Do you value security, sensuality, or service? The list can go on and on. Chances are you value most if not all of these things and much more. The question for you to ponder is "What are the five or ten most important values in my life—the things that give my life a sense of purpose, meaning, and personal fulfillment?" It's not easy to narrow down, but by doing so, you start to define who you really are, what energizes you, what gives you pleasure in life, and what makes your heart sing.

The really revealing question then becomes, "Is the life I'm living right now a reflection of my deepest values?" If the answer is no, or not consistently so, there is an immediate opportunity to bring more satisfaction into your life by consciously choosing to make decisions about what you do and how you do it within the framework of these values. In the fast-paced world we live in these days, it's easy to drift away from a life that is firmly grounded in the things we value. We can get tunnel vision and see only what is right in front of us. Things that are truly important to us can fall by the wayside and may only get our attention in a crisis. In the whirlwind of activity that absorbs us, we can easily get out of balance and shove things on the back burner that should really be priorities. Quality time with our children, date nights with our husband, dinner parties with friends, time to spend in spiritual reflection, volunteering time to those in need, attending continuing education classes, activities that keep our bodies fit and healthy. Burnout results from living a life that is chronically out of sync with our sense of values.

Once you gain clarity about your most important values, it becomes much easier to prioritize how you spend your time. Insights about new directions in life start to come into focus.

Choices and decisions become so much easier when evaluated in the context of your most deeply held values.

Julia reached a point of midlife crisis when the writing was on the wall that her relationship of several years was at a breaking point. The relationship had been fun and had afforded her a life of luxury and leisure. Though she had owned and managed several businesses in the past, she hadn't been working at all since she entered this relationship. She had become restless and itchy to do something that really mattered.

It was at this point that Julia came to me to explore her options and a new direction in life. We worked through an intensive retreat process to explore her deepest desires and values. Among her top ten values were: Fun, Beauty, Freedom, Balance, Creativity, Health and Healing, Sensuality, and Color.

It became rapidly apparent that Julia would be happiest using her entrepreneurial and artistic flair in a business that would promote health and healing using sensual elements and featuring rich and vibrant color. It was important for her to have a spicy balance in her life and to experience fun and freedom in the process of building a business.

The ideas began to flow fast and furious. We looked at options for quite a number of viable business ideas. But one idea rose to the top and it was all Julia could think about and dream about. She let her imagination soar and very quickly her Bouvé® business was born. Bouvés are hats fashioned from soft, sensuous fabrics. You pull them on your head then wrap them around in imaginative and fun ways. At first Julia's focus was on Bouvé as a fashion item for women who value personal style. Very quickly, a whole new market found her. It turns out that the Bouvé is perfect for women who are suffering from hair loss as a result of chemotherapy. It fills a need to not only cover their heads, but also enables them to feel beautiful, stylish, and nurtured as they work through the process of healing.

Through her Bouvé business, Julia has fulfilled both her artistic, creative side and her healing, healthful side as well. The process of exploring and honoring her deepest values became the catalyst that energized Julia to make a series of life-transforming decisions and to launch a successful business that embodies all of her personal strengths and passions. Julia lights up when she talks about her accomplishments. She feels happy and blessed to have a business that is so much fun for her and that fills such a poignant need for women.

What Do You Really Want?

What do you dream of for your life? What do you want for your life more than anything in the world? If time, money, and resources were no object, what would you be doing with your life? Would you embark on a new a career you feel passionate about? Would you bask in a blissful life partner relationship? Would you boldly give expression to your brand of creativity? Would you find a way to make a difference in the world? Would you slow down and just enjoy a peaceful life?

Our fondest dream may be as simple as wanting to live a joyful life or as ambitious as wanting to be rich and famous. Our dreams are personal and as unique as fingerprints. No dream should be discounted as frivolous, silly, or impractical. All dreams are the fuel for propelling ourselves to a more fulfilling life. A word about patience: time is on your side. Never discount a dream because it's not something you can see yourself achieving in a month or a year or even five years. Dreams languish and die due to lack of attention and focus more than anything else. We fail to give our dreams attention and focus because at some level we don't believe they are possible. At this juncture on the journey, Stepping Stone Two, I want you to set aside judgment about any dream you may have tucked away deep inside. Go ahead, shine a light on those dreams you have hidden in your mental closet. Dust off the cobwebs and let your dreams come to the forefront of your mind. Look and see what is in there!

To find those lost dreams, start with remembering who you were as a child: What did you want to be when you grew up? Who did you idolize as a child? Who were your role models? Who are your role models now? Who do you admire the most in terms of their lifestyle, career, social status, contribution, etc? Why? When you were in high school, what did you imagine studying in college? Where did you want to live? What kind of family life, social life, and lifestyle did you imagine you would have? These are clues that will help you begin to resurrect your dreams and begin to form a vision for a future that is joyful, balanced, and fulfilling. Go ahead and let yourself dream!

Permission to Have What You Want

I find that the process of exploring our deepest desires and longings can be a two-edged sword. On the one hand, the process evokes a sense of joy and excitement, giving us a glimpse into possibility. On the other hand, connecting with the ideals and dreams we left behind can be overwhelming and the journey ends for some with the curtain on a possible future slamming shut. A chorus of doubt, fear, sorrow, regret, resentment, and anger can sabotage the process in a heartbeat. We might get caught up in beating ourselves up for making this choice or following that path or abandoning our values or allowing ourselves to be swept up in a life dictated by someone else's choices.

All too often the silent but deadly inner voice that has rerouted our lives from the joyful place of living our dreams is "I don't deserve." Take a moment and close your eyes and ask yourself if you carry around a belief that says, "I don't deserve" or "I am not worthy." If asking the question elicits a tear or two, or a gut-wrenching sadness, then you've got some work to do on this issue. Giving wings to your dreams is going to require you to consciously remove those invisible but ever-present shackles that serve to limit and inhibit you from going for what you really want.

I'm here to give you permission to see yourself as deserving and worthy of whatever your heart desires. Unfortunately, my permission isn't really what you need! It is your own permission that must be granted—from yourself to yourself. A good way to do this is to do some work in your journal. Start by making a list of everything that comes to mind when you say the words, "I want" or "I desire." For example, I want to be successful, I want to have a beautiful home, I desire to feel safe and secure, I desire to have a lot of money.

Then take this list and for each item, create the following series of statements: I deserve to have a beautiful home (or I am worthy of having a beautiful home.) I give myself permission to have a beautiful home. I am open to having a beautiful home. Do this process for as many desires and longings that you can think of. I recommend reading this list out loud for as many days as it takes until you feel a shift occur as you start to actually buy the truth in these statements! To get what you want in life, you must give yourself permission to have it!

This step is crucial in order to short-circuit the flow of self-sabotaging behaviors that come from long-standing negative belief systems we've subconsciously adopted about ourselves. This topic is so important that Stepping Stone Three is dedicated entirely to learning how to recognize your limiting beliefs and consciously shift your beliefs to a more positive place that will support your success in moving in a new direction.

If you are experiencing strong resistance to the idea that you are deserving or worthy of what you desire, I recommend going back to Stepping Stone One and spending more time there before moving on. Stepping Stone One is about empowering yourself with self-love, self-nurturing, and self-acceptance. This is a powerful antidote to counter the deeply ingrained feelings of "I don't deserve" and "I'm not worthy." Did you skip over those activities suggested in Stepping Stone One? If so, do not pass Go! These stepping stones build on each other. Please don't short-change yourself. The ultimate outcome is to see yourself in a new light—as a woman of strength, confidence, courage and conviction—capable of successfully navigating the journey from lost to found. Take all the time you need. Your dreams are yours when you are ready.

Part II:

Creating an Inner Environment for Your Dreams to Flourish

"We cannot discover

new oceans unless we

have the courage to lose

sight of the shore"

–Unknown

◆ Stepping Stone Three:

Believing You Can Have What You Want

Conquering your inner critic and limiting beliefs

> *"The future belongs to those who believe
> in the beauty of their dreams."*
>
> –Eleanor Roosevelt

No matter how deeply you desire your dream to manifest, limiting beliefs about yourself and your abilities will stop you cold in your quest to achieve that dream. Negative, limiting belief systems tend to operate unconsciously, creating patterns of experience that repeatedly disappoint us in their outcome. It is only when we choose to become conscious about our belief systems and proactively seek to reprogram our thinking that new and more desirable patterns and outcomes can occur.

Many of us were taught as children that when we think highly of ourselves, we've grown "too big for our britches" or we will get "a big head." I, for one, didn't care for the idea of having my head explode! As little girls we were often taught to be self-deprecating, and to deny our personal power and gifts in order to ensure that people would like us and not be threatened by our strength. Over time, these external messages become deeply held belief systems that serve to limit us in profound ways. One of the biggest show-stoppers that gets in the way of realizing our dreams is a simple yet pervasive, negative belief. Two deceptively small words: "I can't."

The "I Can't Monster"

I came face-to-face with my own "I can't monster" when I was recovering from stress and trauma during my medical leave of absence. It was the late spring when I attended a weekend work-shop on the California Mendocino Coast. The workshop was held in a vacation home at the rustic and beautiful Sea Ranch commu-nity, where we could view sea lions nursing their pups along the shoreline. It was a perfect setting for nurturing myself and doing some serious soul-searching.

As the workshop got under way, we were asked to pick a single issue or problem we were grappling with in our lives as our focus for the weekend. Immediately, I felt overwhelmed and lost because I couldn't think of a single issue to focus on that didn't threaten to drown me in its magnitude. I burst into tears, feeling I had failed even before we'd begun.

Sensitive to my obvious pain, our facilitator called for a break and took me aside in another room. She gently began to ask me questions and to probe for what was at the root of my upset. She intuited by our quiet talk that a productive focus for me for the weekend would be to tackle my deeply entrenched belief around the idea that "I can't."

A bit surprised, I asked, "That's it? You want me to focus on 'I can't,' and nothing else?" It seemed like a pretty wimpy focus for an entire weekend, considering all the other issues in my life. She said, "Trust me on this. I suggest you start by writing in your journal all the ways in which you tell yourself you can't." So that is exactly what I did. The workshop included plenty of unstructured time to wander in nature and enjoy the magnificent Pacific coastline. During my free time, I headed off with my notebook and pen to find a quiet spot on the ocean. I climbed up and over jagged rocks until I found a totally private little cove where I could be alone with my thoughts, and began to journal about "I can't." I was astonished as I scribbled furiously and continuously for what seemed like an hour. My "I can't" list ran on for four full pages!

As I studied what I had written down, a realization dawned on me. I had been subconsciously operating under the false belief that I was powerless to take control of my life. I saw clearly that the core of my belief system was grounded in the truth of past circumstances in my life in which I truly had no control, and "I can't" was a statement of fact.

Somehow, those facts had expanded and gotten embellished over time to become a pervasive, mind-boggling, and paralyzing belief system. Boiled down to a few core themes, the beliefs now were: "I can't be happy," "I can't learn anything new," "I can't take care of myself," "I can't be healthy and fit," "I can't be seen or heard," "I can't be loved the way I want to be loved," and "I can't say what I really think and feel because others will not like me."

As the ridiculousness of all this set in and I saw the very tiny and limiting box I had created for myself, I laughed out loud. I saw a glimpse of the incredible freedom that opened up for me by simply letting go of these limiting beliefs! In that moment I ripped out those four pages and began a new list in my journal, this time a four-page list of things "I can" do in my life. As I did this, I felt my energy soar and an experience of incredible joy and positive anticipation welled up in me for the new life that lay ahead.

Oh Yes I Can!

When I rejoined the workshop group back at the house, I shared my discovery about how my life had been under the control of my "I can't monster." The other participants joined me in celebrating the breakthrough I had achieved. On the next day of the workshop, I consciously chose a deliberate, visible way to send a message to my "I can't monster," and showed up for the workshop wearing no makeup. You got it, one of my silly "I can't" messages had been: "I can't go out in public without my makeup on," as if people would run and hide from the horror of it! It was truly an uncomfortable thing for me to do, but I persevered and was glad I did. It was a first step in overriding my limiting beliefs and getting control of my life.

As part of the workshop, our group took a little field trip down the road to visit the Sea Ranch Chapel, a unique piece of architecture, constructed by local artisans in memorial to a young artist. It was a riot of textures and colors: Wood mixed with iron, stained glass windows, mosaics and tapestries in abundance. We all went inside together for a meditation experience. Not being one who was adept at closing my eyes and achieving a meditative state, I chose to sit quietly and drink in visually the exquisite work of art that the chapel was.

I started to write in my journal, reconnecting with my little-girl self who loved colorful things. I started writing about my love of art glass, kaleidoscopes, stained glass windows, and such. Suddenly, I got this overwhelming, loud urge to write the words "DON'T

TOUCH!" I was startled. My little-girl self was pouting, saying to herself, this is so beautiful, but "I can't touch."

A powerful surge of energy came over me and I said quietly and definitively to myself: "OH YES I CAN!" I got up from my bench in the chapel and walked up to the stained glass window in front and began to run my hands over the beautiful glass. (I'm getting goose bumps as I remember this!) Slowly I made my way around the entire chapel, running my hands over the different textures, feeling the roughness and warmth of the wood, the cold and hard wrought iron, the dips and jagged edges of the mosaics, the silkiness of the tapestries. Throughout my exploration, there were tears of joy streaming down my cheeks.

My companions at the chapel came out of their meditations to quietly observe the profound experience I was having. When I went back to my seat, it felt like electricity was running through my hands and I was completely mute. I could not say a word. I walked out of that chapel a different woman. I had slain my "I can't monster."

Dealing With Your Inner Critic

If you are going to be in charge of your own life, it is important to get a handle on just what those insidious messages are that swirl around inside you. Without your conscious intention to do something about them, these negative beliefs will continue to enjoy free reign inside your brain, throwing up massive barriers to limit your ability to create productive change in your life.

The very best way to handle negative beliefs is to cut them off at the knees by just noticing that they are there. Become an observer of your own mental dialog and pay attention to the silent messages of your inner critic. When you do, simply say to it: "Thank you for sharing," and consciously replace that thought with an empowering message that enables you to shift into a more positive mental attitude. In essence, you want to fire your inner critic and hire an inner coach! For some, it helps to personify the inner critic. I imagine mine as an impish little gremlin that sits on my shoulder, so when I notice him, I can just kind of mentally flick him off!

If you listen closely, you will notice that the voice of the inner gremlin speaks in the language of victimhood, of powerlessness, and of neediness. In order to shift into more powerful, positive thinking, you must stop thinking of yourself as a victim and embrace the idea that you have the freedom to choose. You can remain stuck in old patterns and beliefs about yourself, or you can choose to create a new and improved story of your life, a story that acknowledges the gifts and lessons of your life rather than the pain and the limitations. Make up your mind to own your personal power and take charge of your life!

Learning to shift your inner language as well as your verbal language is key to moving away from feeling powerless about your life. Here are some examples of how a change in your choice of words can shift your energy to a more confident and self-assured stance:

Replace	With
I should	I choose to, I desire to, I want to
I need to	It's important to me to
I have to	I desire to
I can't	I can or I'm not willing to
I'll try	I intend to
I always, I never	I sometimes, In the past, I

Take a moment to try out these phrases in a sentence and pay attention to your shift in energy when you say it one way versus the other. The left-hand column reflects a feeling of having no control and no power to choose, whereas the right-hand column will serve to empower you. It may seem like a subtle distinction at first glance, but your choice of words, how you talk to yourself, and how you talk about yourself does make a big difference. It's a powerful way to begin to reprogram your negative belief system.

Letting Go of Past Beliefs Consciously

Become conscious that the past is just that—*it is in the past.* Today is a new day and a clean slate on which to build the rest of your life! When you dwell on past disappointments, you are actually projecting more of the same into your future. How often do you hear yourself saying, "I never" or "I always," as a way of discounting the possibility of generating a new outcome for yourself?

The following are examples of statements that will leave you feeling hopeless and helpless. "I never succeed at implementing my ideas." "I always get disappointed when I try to change." "I never get interviews." "I always work for such jerks." "I never get what I want." "I always screw things up." "I never meet interesting men." "I always date selfish men." This list could go on and on, but the important thing is to become aware of how you think about your past experiences and whether you have unconsciously (or consciously!) drawn conclusions about yourself that limit your possibilities. Remember: What you think about is what you tend to bring about.

What you tell yourself is what drives the outcomes in your life. When you recognize a powerful belief about yourself that is grounded in past experience, restate the belief to both acknowledge the past and to state your intention to create a new reality in the present and future. For example, say to yourself: "In the past, I have dated only selfish men...Going forward, I will make healthier choices." Or, "In the past, I have experienced failure in implementing my ideas...Going forward, I choose to stay focused and committed to bringing my ideas to fruition."

At any point in time, you have the power to re-invent yourself. The first step is to make peace with the past. Accept your past experiences and choices as the best you were able to do at the time given your knowledge, beliefs, and circumstances. Look upon the past as a fertile ground for learning about what works and what doesn't work for you in your life. Be compassionate with yourself and let go of judgment about past choices. Forgive yourself and others for being less than perfect human beings. Accept the past for whatever it is and choose a new, improved path for the future!

We often fall into the trap of black and white thinking, of going to extremes in judging ourselves or setting expectations for ourselves. There is a vast continuum between black and white, a myriad of shades of gray to experiment with and try on for size. In thinking about the past, it is helpful to refrain from labeling it as "right" or "wrong." You might think of a past experience where you did not perform as competently as you thought you should, therefore, you judged yourself as incompetent, when in fact you were just somewhere along the continuum of a learning experience, on your way to becoming more competent.

When I was in high school, I used to make my parents crazy over the fits of hysteria I would have if I didn't think I was going to get an A on a test or report. In my mind, if I didn't study or work hard enough to make that A, I was sure I was going to fail. I was such a perfectionist that the continuum between A and F was completely obscured for me. We could all benefit from cutting ourselves some slack and opening our minds to be okay with the shades of gray that are available to us so we can relax more and enjoy the process of living our lives.

One Step At a Time

As you work to re-invent the way you think about yourself and build a more empowering belief system to support you, notice the resistance that comes up from inside of you. The inner gremlin can throw a fit and attempt to become even more entrenched, digging its heels in for the long haul. It is common for people in this process to become confronted with strong negative emotion as they begin taking on their inner critic. They'll hear the litany: "Yeah, right!" "Who do you think you are?" "Who are you fooling?" "You are such a fraud!" "Dream on, girlfriend!"

Because of the tenacity of your inner gremlin, it's important to set your expectations that shifting your deeply held beliefs about yourself is not an overnight activity. Take it easy and recognize that you will go through stages. The idea is to chip away at the negative programming. It is actually more effective to approach your inner gremlin gently rather than attempting to annihilate it in a one-two punch. In essence, any attempts at reprogramming will fail, if, at some level, you cannot believe what you are saying to be true or possible.

Caroline was perpetually down on herself. Her inner critic would berate her by saying "You are such a flake! You never finish anything you start. You've got your head in the clouds—all these great ideas and no action. You make terrible decisions."

Caroline was an artist at heart and was full of creative ideas. She had a passion for finding a way to bring art experiences to children, yet the possibility of actually doing this was feeling like a pipe dream to her. I had suggested she work with an affirmation that said simply, "I believe in me!" She literally started to quake. Her inner gremlin went into freak-out mode. So we calmed her down and I acknowledged that this was too big for her to take on right now. I worked with her to find a less threatening statement that would move her in that direction and be something she could fully believe. We came up with this statement: "I have great creative ideas and I am learning to trust and believe in myself." Caroline's energy shifted immediately, as she embraced this new statement.

Over time, small steps in the direction of reprogramming your belief system will lead to a huge transformation in the way you think and believe about yourself. It requires persistence, focus, and attention. It is most powerful to write down your new statements of belief or affirmation and to keep them in a place where you will frequently notice them. Just writing it down or saying it out loud once is helpful, but if you leave it at that, not much is going to shift. The negative beliefs are too firmly entrenched to surrender that easily. This process requires repetition and more repetition.

I recommend using note cards or sticky notes to post your new empowering belief statements where you will see them frequently. Decide to say them out loud at certain times of the day for reinforcement. Repeat this one idea to yourself throughout the day for as many days as it takes, until you feel like you truly embrace it as your new truth. Then up the ante! Make it even more emphatic or move on to a new and more challenging belief.

You Are What You Believe

Whatever statement you put after the two words *I am* becomes a statement of your reality. Is it going to be a statement of limitation or a statement of expansive possibility? Just know that whichever it is, you are going to be right. You are what you believe yourself to be. It doesn't matter whether you say it out loud or not. How you think about yourself in terms of *I am* is what drives your choices and either propels you forward productively or holds you behind some imaginary line that you can't seem to cross over to get to happiness. Do you say to yourself, "*I am* such a loser," or do you say to yourself, "*I am* courageous and I learn from my experiences, good and bad." Do you say to yourself, "*I am* not worthy" or do you say to yourself, "*I am* loving and lovable, deserving of all the good things I desire for my life"?

Sonia and I were working to create a vision statement that would empower her to embark on a major career transition that included a move back to her home state and starting her own retail business focused on gathering treasures from around the world. A delightful woman with an almost childlike sense of wonder, she had a long and successful career in corporate management, and a variety of creative talents and interests.

We had spent several hours brainstorming and uncovering a long list of gifts, talents, passions, interests, and traits that described who Sonia was in rich and expansive detail. Referring to this long list of words and phrases, I asked her to create a statement beginning with the words "I am." As I stood at the flipchart with my marker poised to capture her beauty on paper, I was stunned by the words that poured definitively from her mouth. "I am an alcoholic." Though she had not touched alcohol in years, this still was the overriding definition of how she saw herself.

Labeling yourself—I am ADD (Attention Deficient Disorder), or I am an alcoholic—is a common trap to be aware of. Though these may be true statements, they are NOT the totality of who you are! You are much bigger than any self-limiting label. These are challenges to live with, to be sure, but who you are is so much greater than a single diagnosis. Labeling yourself in reference to your limitations puts the focus on what you cannot do and creates a closed box in which you get to conduct your life. Instead, see yourself in all your glory. If you are someone who has ADD or who struggles with alcohol or other addictions, it's very likely you have incredible gifts and talents that have been denied expression. What a gift to give yourself, to expand your definition of who you are, and tell yourself, "I am creative and multifaceted," or "I am talented and have gifts I have yet to share."

Another common label that many of us are saddled with is "I am afraid." Fear is often the silent culprit behind our inability to move forward. It might be fear of taking risks, fear of change, fear of rejection, fear of failure, and even fear of success. You can think about FEAR in one of two ways, Forgetting Everything's All Right or Forget Everything And Run! Which are you going to choose?

Feel The Fear...And Do It Anyway

Fear reigns supreme when your belief system is focused on disempowering thoughts such as, "I can't, It's not possible, I'm not good enough." Many years ago I read Susan Jeffers' best-selling book *Feel the Fear and Do It Anyway*. This was one of those life-changing books for me. I love the way she boiled it all down to say that the underlying issue behind fear was the belief that "I can't handle it."

I used to have so many fears that fear was more in control of my life than I was. When I first learned to drive, I was terrified of driving on the freeways, a fear that I inherited from my mother. I stayed completely clear of freeways until one day when I was twenty years old, my boss insisted that I run an errand on the other side of Houston. Houston is huge. You simply can't get across town without navigating the freeway system. I remember feeling nearly paralyzed with fear and hearing the voice screaming inside me, "I can't do that!" I had no choice but to do it anyway, if I wanted to keep my job. Once I experienced freeway driving and found that I could indeed survive, well, hey, I never worried about that particular fear again. Sometimes, you just have to push through the fears to get to the other side.

Amanda found it very freeing to face her fears head on. Amanda had just celebrated her fiftieth birthday when she came to work with me as her coach. She was feeling that her life was slipping away from her. Never married, she had fallen into the role of caretaker in her family. She lived with her elderly, ailing parents and often took on the role of surrogate mother for a young friend, as well.

Amanda longed for a more carefree life, to have travel adventures, to express herself through painting and writing, and to simply be able to say "No" to the relentless demands that seemed to constrict her choices. She was fearful of stepping out of her safe but secluded world, yet she yearned to "color outside the lines." Her biggest fear was to let people see what she considered her "irresponsible" side. She feared that personal rejection would follow if she asserted her own needs and set boundaries with her family. She had repressed her own needs to the point of succumbing to a stress-related illness.

As I coached her, Amanda began to take some small steps to face her fears. She carved out time for herself to take art classes each week and to write in her journal every day. She began to say "Yes" to her longings to visit art museums and take occasional weekend trips. She began to say "No" to small requests, and eventually found she could say "No" with confidence, rather than compromising commitments she had made to herself.

Amanda faced her fears and found she not only gained more joy and well-being in her life, but that her relationships with the important people around her strengthened as she began to show up as her true self. She expressed the result of facing her fears in her own words: "Now, instead of being cloistered behind my imaginary walls, I am flying high on the trapeze of life—and I like it!"

Get Off Your Own Back!

Our unconscious negative belief systems can wreak havoc in our lives. The voices of the external naysayers of our childhood have taken up residence inside us where they have become more brutal and persistent than the original messengers ever were. In short, we've become quite expert at beating ourselves up, berating ourselves for mistakes of the past and throwing nasty barbs at ourselves when we dare think outside of the box we've become accustomed to operating in. I know, because I've had a particularly nasty, mean-mouthed inner critic to deal with most of my life. I was a relentless perfectionist, on myself like a quarter horse with a whip, always driving myself to do things better.

A compassionate therapist once asked me to contemplate this question: "How would you treat a good friend who was having a challenge like this?" or "What would you say to a friend who was beating herself up like that?" Of course, the answer was: I'd be kinder and less demanding. Then I had to face the logical next question: "What if you treated yourself as nicely and with as much compassion as you treat your friends?"

I had always been a very caring and compassionate person where my family and friends were concerned. I would have been the first one to console and to cheer on someone who was feeling down on herself, to point out the positives in a situation and remind them that they did the best they could at the time. It had never occurred to me to treat myself with the same caring and compassion when I made a mistake or a misstep. Learning to be gentle with myself has taken time and persistence, but it has been an essential step toward finding joy in my life.

Margo came to me as she was facing the prospect of an empty nest. She was in her early fifties, and had nearly completed the job of getting her four lovely children off to college. She had been a dedicated stay-at-home mother for over twenty years. I had the opportunity to become acquainted with her children and I must say I was deeply impressed with these four extraordinary young men and women. A job well done!

The only problem was that Margo was completely disgusted with how she herself had turned out. She was a good fifty pounds overweight, wearing clothes she despised, taking no care to style her hair, and feeling her marriage was crumbling. She considered herself personally a failure. She was relentless in berating herself for what she saw as her lack of personal discipline.

When I asked her how she would treat one of her children who was facing such a challenge, Margo experienced a profound shift. I asked her to consider focusing her immensely gifted talent for parenting onto herself. As she contemplated this idea, I saw her face soften and her shoulders relax and an expression of peace come across her face for the first time. Margo had believed she was not worthy of her own time and attention. As she worked on consciously shifting this belief and treating herself with the same compassion she had for her own children, the extra pounds began to melt off with relative ease, and she began to experience a great deal more joy in her life.

It's Okay to Ask for Help

One limiting belief that is common among women and tends to keep us stuck in frustration and overwhelm, is the idea that "I should be able to do everything myself." There seems to be a great deal of inner chatter in the way for most of us to allow ourselves the luxury of asking for help of any kind. Many of us have been conditioned to believe that it is not polite to ask for what we want, or that it is a sign of weakness to ask for help. Others may not ask because they fear being told "No," and the feeling of rejection that comes with it. Some have perfected the art of the hint and indulge in passive-aggressive behavior if we don't get what we want. Few are comfortable with asking directly for what we want. It's a jumbled-up mess of fearful, negative thinking that gets in the way of asking.

Whatever the reason, many of us trudge along and continually struggle rather than seek assistance from others. How many of us tend to pout if our partners don't give us what we want? Could it be that we have neglected to ask? Is it any wonder that men are exasperated with women for expecting them to be mind readers or experts at deciphering the hint? How many of us carry over that tendency into other relationships in life? It's no wonder many women develop a pervasive belief that says, "I never seem to get what I want in life."

I have heard so many stories about people who have reached the depths of despair and only then called out to a Higher Power to ask for help. And then they experience an answer to their call and wonder why it took them so long to ask! Or on a more human level, often times, a woman on the verge of divorce with nothing to lose, will finally state clearly what she wants and her husband, eager to make her happy and to avoid losing her, bends over backwards to give it to her. Then a light bulb goes on and she realizes all she had to do to make her needs known, was to ask.

Asking is another muscle that needs to be exercised. Shift into believing that what you want, and what you need, is there for the asking. If your "That would be selfish" voice is piping up, I'm not surprised. But think, wouldn't you be inclined to help someone who asked for something from you? And if you were not able to give what was asked for, wouldn't you try to help find someone who could? By all means, continue to be a giving person, but also be open to allowing yourself to receive from others.

If it is better to give than to receive, doesn't it follow that allowing someone to give to you, is allowing her to feel good about herself? By receiving, you are allowing someone else the positive experience of giving. It goes both ways! For the most part, people give because they want to and because it makes them feel good, not because they feel an obligation. Refusing to allow someone to give to you is denying her the right to feel good about helping you.

If you ask for something and the answer is no, let that be okay. Perhaps you have asked the wrong person or the person doesn't presently have the resources to give you what you need. Find someone else and ask again.

When looking for a new job, after staying home with my kids for seven years, I was given a slip of paper by a women's career resource center. It had fifty words on it: forty-nine "No's" and one "Yes." The point was to cross off a "No" every time you interviewed for a job and got rejected. The visual was very powerful—with every "No," you were that much closer to "Yes!" I think the fear of rejection is universal. The secret is to learn that "No" is not about you, it is about the other party, for whatever reason, being unable to accommodate your request. It doesn't mean that your request is not worthy, it only means that you haven't found the right fit.

Whether you need to ask for a job or ask for directions, it is important to ask in a clear, direct way with a positive expectation for an affirmative, helpful response. Be alert to your inner belief system that may be professing that you don't deserve to get what you want. If this is an issue with you, work on shifting into a positive expectation that you are worthy to receive what you ask for.

Again, be clear about what you want so that you can articulate your request effectively. We all know the story of Aladdin's Lamp, and one might come away with the moral of the story being that you must be careful what you ask for! Yes, it is important to be conscious about what we ask for because there is magic in the asking. Fortunately, unlike with Aladdin's Lamp, we are not restricted to only three wishes in life.

Empower yourself to ask for assistance whether from a friend, your partner, a work associate, an acquaintance, or even a perfect stranger if circumstances warrant. If you believe in a Higher Power, empower yourself to ask for assistance from the power you consider to be greater than yourself. Always ask in a positive, upbeat manner. To ask does not mean to beg! It is said that the most effective prayer is a prayer of gratitude. Ask with an attitude of positive expectation and an expression of heart-felt appreciation and watch as doors open, resources appear, and amazing coincidences show up to make it easy to get what you want.

When You Sincerely Believe

I cannot overemphasize the importance of moving away from negative and limiting belief systems in order to create positive change in your life. What you believe about yourself—your character, your abilities, your worthiness, your trustworthiness, your ability to choose—has the power to either change your life in profound ways or to keep you stuck in patterns that create perpetual misery and unhappiness. If you are meeting up with too much resistance, and are unable to shift your inner critic on your own, consider working with a life coach to hold your hand and guide you through the process.

Most of all, I ask that you be patient with yourself. We are talking about a lifetime of accumulated belief systems that are complex and well defended. Time is on your side. All you need to do is decide that you are worth it, and make a commitment to stay present to your inner critic and persistent in your resolve to create a kinder, gentler, more empowering inner coach. Transform your inner voice from one that stops you to one that cheers you on and brings you home to the life you want. Give yourself permission to experience life in a new and empowering way.

Learning to recognize and consciously replace negative self-talk is the first step toward opening the door to an abundance of positive feeling—not the least of which is self-love and appreciation. From there you will find the path to achieving greater joy, inner peace, contentment and a general upbeat outlook on life. In Stepping Stone Four, you'll learn how to consciously reach for positive feeling so that you can begin to transform the quality of your life right now.

Feeling Your Way To A Better Life

Finding joy in the journey

> *"Happiness is not a station you arrive at,*
> *but a manner of traveling."*
>
> –Margaret Lee Runbeck

It was January of 2000, the beginning of the new millennium, and I was aware that my new life was being birthed as well. I was standing in a circle, holding hands with fifteen other kindred spirits, feeling the electric charge of positive energy flowing between us. We stood under the massive redwoods on a ranch in the Santa Cruz Mountains, feeling embraced by Mother Nature herself. We were taking turns, going around the circle, expressing our gratitude for the experience we just shared. We had come for a weekend retreat with hopes and dreams, and we were all leaving with a conviction that what we wanted was within our reach.

We had immersed ourselves in a weekend of *positive thought and feeling*. It was an extraordinary experience, a natural high, and a shared exuberance for the beauty of the moment, as well as a joyful anticipation of the future. Each of us had our own unique vision of what would bring us happiness. For some it was the miracle of robust health, for others it was the dream of attracting a loving and supportive life partner, for others it was a desire to find that perfect job or career that would bring both personal satisfaction and quality of life. Others, for whom it seemed nothing in life was working, sought the means to raise themselves from the pits of depression to enjoy a full and joyful life, complete with good health, satisfying relationships, and financial success.

Without exception, we all left the ranch feeling buoyed by hope and a deep connection to a world of possibility, as we began to see ourselves as empowered masters of our own destinies, fueled by our newfound awareness that you can actually feel your way to a better life, by tuning into the pleasures of the moment and finding joy in the journey.

My Epiphany

Just prior to attending this uplifting weekend retreat, I reached a moment of truth where my job was concerned. I had been back at work for about eight months, working only part-time hours, as I was still trying to fully regain my health and well-being. During the Christmas holidays, I had found peace and serenity while vacationing at a beautiful Caribbean beach resort. It was a temporary bliss. As I returned to my job, sitting at my desk, dealing with the backlog of email and the crises du jour, I had the epiphany.

It was January 5, 2000. "I can't do this any more!" The message came through loud and clear and it was non-negotiable. I decided in that moment that I could no longer work there; the job and the work environment were stressful and not conducive to my healing journey. The contrast between how I felt on vacation and the way

I felt after only twenty minutes back at my desk created an opportunity to make a powerful choice. I began to look at new possibilities. Having tasted the benefits of part-time work, I wanted to find something new that I enjoyed, and that would offer financial rewards with freedom and flexible hours.

I began to consider an idea that I had continually pushed away—working as an independent marketing consultant. "That's too risky!" I told myself, "I'm a single mom. It would be crazy to take that kind of chance." But the tug was stronger than my resistance. I began searching the web for independent consultant opportunities.

The practical side of me insisted that I also check job listings for the possibility of a new position with my current employer. Here's where listening to my intuition was instructive. As I pulled up the list of job openings, I felt a knot tighten in my stomach and a feeling of deep dread come over me. As I viewed the independent consulting opportunities, I felt a surge of excitement and joyful anticipation. The right choice was revealed and I became determined to set out on my own. I wanted to enjoy the freedom of being my own boss and to have the flexibility to spend more time with my kids. I was a woman on a mission, armed with clarity and conviction.

Following my intuition, I signed up with a top-notch placement agency for marketing consultants. Within a few weeks, I landed an offer for a long-term consulting assignment. Not only that, my contract was with a high-tech industry giant, which at the time, was by far the most coveted assignment available through the agency.

I took the leap and quit my salaried job and just reveled in the freedom and joy of my new work. That year, I made more money than I had ever made in a salaried job, and I made it working the part-time hours of my choosing, working with people who really appreciated and valued me. This transition was ideal for me. I was still working in high-tech marketing, leveraging my fifteen years of experience, and I had removed myself from a work environment that had been draining my energy. My health and well-being became a non-issue. I felt better, mentally and physically, than I had in a very long time.

How can you know if you are making the right decision in the moment? By learning to trust and respect your intuition. If it *feels* good, do it! We are born with an incredibly powerful guidance system, our intuition, which becomes disabled over time when our fears and negative inner critic have been allowed to rule. That's why the work in Stepping Stone Three is so vitally important. Clearing out habitual negativity makes the space for your intuition to rise to the forefront; you can learn to easily discern between something that *feels right* for you and something that *feels wrong* for you.

I used to have a tough time recognizing the difference between when my intuition was trying to tell me that something wasn't right for me, and when I was just succumbing to fear, because my fear was pretty much a constant, overshadowing everything else. Unbridled fear can completely obliterate an intuitive nudge trying to guide you in a new direction. It's an experiential process. In time and with practice, you'll learn to trust how you *feel*.

In retrospect, some might be tempted to judge my choice to become a marketing consultant as a distraction or a detour. After all, it's clear *now* that my purpose in life wasn't to stay in high-tech marketing! However, I have learned, and I encourage my clients to accept, that the best way to travel between point A and point B isn't necessarily a straight line! Sometimes you need a staging platform, a transition space, so to speak, to better prepare yourself to move in a radically new direction. At the time, I still had not discovered what I really wanted to do with my life. What I was sure of, was that it was important to improve *the quality of my life* in order to regain my health and well-being.

Sometimes the first priority has to be to get yourself out of a toxic environment, whether at home or at the office, in the most expeditious way possible. In this circumstance, any change is a good change as long as you are moving yourself in a positive direction and not just jumping from one bad situation to another.

It is very comforting to know that the answer to the question "How do I get there from here?" (and *there* might be only a vague yearning for a better life) may include stops at multiple ports of call along the journey. Some of these stops may be unplanned and it may be unclear how they connect. I have found my intuition to be a reliable guide on the journey. As long as you keep your eye on your ultimate desire and commit to choosing what *feels* right and what works for you in the here and now, you can relax and enjoy the adventures as they unfold along the way to your ultimate destination.

The wonderful thing about trusting intuition is that you don't have to figure everything out. You don't have to be able to see exactly what will happen next on your journey. You can just go with the flow. The truth is, most of us can't even imagine the fullest extent of what is possible. Going with the flow means trusting that the outcome of your efforts may well exceed the specifics of your imagination (and may even look wildly different from what you envision!)

It's the feeling experience we are really trying to achieve. The specifics of our dreams are what we *think* we need to make us *feel* happy, content, joyful, at peace, and loved. Think about it: if what you achieve is a state of happiness, contentment, joy, peace and love, wouldn't you have to concede that you've got everything that is truly important? What if you could create a feeling place like this from which to conduct your journey? To *feel good* right now, no matter what your specific circumstances, that is the goal. What we want to do is to short-circuit the "I'll be happy when..." syndrome. The real win is to enjoy the journey.

The Power of Positive Feeling

Positive feelings such as joy, love, peace, harmony, happiness, excitement, and acceptance create a profound sense of well-being. In fact, just thinking about positive emotions will likely put a smile on your face. When you consciously dwell in positive feeling, you will find that you attract more positive people, experiences, and circumstances into your life. Positive people like to be around other positive people. When you are looking at your world through a positive filter, you tend to see more that is positive in your world. It's like when you are thinking of buying a new car—you suddenly see the model you are interested in everywhere! Your experience of life reflects where you put your focus. It's a choice whether you dwell on what's wrong in your life or whether you focus on what's right and what's possible.

Some people resist this concept and you might be familiar with the remark, "Oh stop being such a Pollyanna!" *Pollyanna* is the name of a movie about a little girl who spread joy by always choosing to see the bright side of a situation, finding the hope when others felt despair, and looking for the gift in negative circumstances. Pollyanna was relentless in her heartfelt joyful expression of life. Some people are downright suspicious of the authenticity of that kind of consistent positive feeling! You might guess that I have some personal experience with this. I've been called a Pollyanna more than a few times in my life, and unfortunately it wasn't meant as a compliment!

The truth is, it is not the circumstances of your life that define the quality of your life it's how you react to them that will create your experience. There are of course events and moments in life that bring on sadness, despair, disappointment, and a whole array of emotions that are not happy ones. And it is certainly important not to bury these very real and vital feelings. It is important to let yourself process strong negative emotions and let them run their natural course in order to heal. However, the damage is done when you allow yourself to get stuck in a never-ending litany of gloomy expectations.

The real culprit that keeps us stuck and unable to move forward is the negative emotion that leaves us in a chronic state of bitterness and victimhood. I'm sure you know people who are the anti-Pollyanna, who seem deeply entrenched in their view of the world as a harsh and unyieldingly painful place. I remember being in a workshop, when I was in my own process of healing, with a woman who was deeply attached to her pain and her belief that life was just one misery after another. My attempts to find a positive spin on her situation didn't just fall on deaf ears—she lashed out at me with such verbal vehemence, I felt as if I'd been physically slapped. With a voice dripping with contempt, she said, "You just want everyone to be happy!" Well if that's a crime, I confess!

Not everyone is ready to move on in life and I have learned that you can't "make" another person happy. The motivation has to come from within. I trust by the fact that you are reading this book that you are indeed motivated and ready to shift your life into a happy and fulfilling place.

The culture around us encourages a chronic kind of complaining about the trials and tribulations of getting through our day. You need look no further than popular sitcoms, which often trade in negative humor and the clever put-down, to see how we are conditioned to look at life through dark-colored glasses. There is a pervasive tendency to look at our world from the perspective of the glass being half-empty rather than half-full. Viewing the world through a lens of positive emotion, if you aren't already accustomed to doing so, will take some practice and some perseverance. After all, it's a muscle that's out of shape and will require some personal training!

What you think about tends to color your perception of reality. It's really a choice whether to view the world as a friendly, supportive place, or to view it as a war zone fraught with battles to wage, forcing you to focus on surviving rather than thriving. If your thoughts are steeped in negative expectations and your feelings awash with gloom and doom, your reality will be one of never-ending struggle and pity parties.

If you are feeling unhappy about your work situation, your home life, your relationship, your health or any other aspect of your life, bring your focus back to what is working rather than what is not working. This will bring you to a more positive feeling place very quickly and uplift your energy to experience life as a friendlier place to be!

Lisa spent four days in a private retreat with me in Santa Barbara. She arrived feeling absolutely miserable and trapped in a job that had her feeling tied up in knots. She was physically tired, mentally anguished, and emotionally steeped in negativity. Contractually, she was bound to stay with her employer for another eighteen months, or be required to reimburse them for her quite substantial moving expenses. Her choice was to stay until the end of her contract.

Working in a man's world, she felt she had fallen victim to an old boys' network that was not only conspiring to hold her back, the men around her were systematically taking credit for everything she had produced for the organization. She was angry, resentful, and feeling completely helpless to do anything about it.

We spent time working to diffuse and release her anger and resentment and to shift her focus onto things she could control. She saw how her situation could in fact be reframed in a more positive light. Once she worked through the negativity, she began to see that she was in fact building a top-notch resume of experience that would position her very well for the next move in her career. She became excited when she realized she did have choices about how to spend her time within the context of her current job that would benefit her down the road.

In order to shift into a more positive feeling state, she began to consciously look for things to appreciate about her current job. Instead of dwelling on the shortcomings of the men she worked with, she began to acknowledge to herself the ways in which she was learning from them. Instead of continuing to beat her head against the wall, she began to accept the situation for what it was, and stopped attaching her feelings of self-worth to whether or not she received acknowledgment for her contributions at work.

Lisa chose to put more effort into building a balanced life for herself, and putting energy into taking small steps that would position her well for the next steps in her long-term plan. Suddenly the situation at work no longer seemed so dire and gloomy. She began to show up with a cheery disposition. Nothing changed in terms of the attitudes and behavior of the men she worked with; however, she no longer allowed the situation to impact her sense of well-being. She found the way to *feel good now* in spite of her exasperating circumstances.

Tapping Into Positive Feeling

How do you go about shifting into positive thought and feeling? Most of us aren't in the habit of calling up positive feeling on demand! One of the fastest and most effective ways to connect with positive feeling is to focus on gratitude. Think about it. It is not possible to feel negative emotion at the same time you are expressing gratitude!

Take a moment now to think about something you feel grateful for in your life. Close your eyes and really embrace the experience of gratitude. Perhaps you are feeling grateful for the warmth of your husband's body as you share your bed at night, or the great big squeezy hugs you get from your children as you tuck them into bed, or you might be so very grateful for your health and physical mobility. Maybe you are grateful for the love of your family. If things aren't going so well for you personally, focus on the world around you. Perhaps you are grateful for the beauty of nature and the crispness of the clean air you breathe in the mountains or at the ocean. You might be grateful for the scent of flowers or the decadent taste of chocolate! Are you grateful to be alive, to experience the unfolding of each new day?

Find an expression of gratitude that is meaningful to you and immerse yourself in the feeling. Notice any shift in your outlook. Gratitude instantly uplifts us. Embrace gratitude as part of your daily routine, right up there with brushing your teeth, and observe the shift in your energy. Notice the difference in the ease of getting through your days when you have expressed gratitude versus the days you let slip by without being conscious of what you appreciate. Consider keeping a gratitude journal or incorporating expressions of gratitude in your daily journaling practice. This simple awareness and conscious choice will work wonders in bringing you to a consistent place of positive feeling about your life.

As you are working with expressing your gratitude, don't forget to include all the qualities that you appreciate about yourself! As we discussed in Stepping Stone Three, so many of us make a habit of focusing on what's wrong with us rather than what is right. We fall victim to a relentless internal bashing for the ways we perceive that we fall short. This is a major culprit in feeling discontent and unhappiness with our lives.

What I would like you to do right now, is to get out your journal and fill at least one entire page with a list of the wonderful qualities that you appreciate about yourself. For example: I appreciate my playful sense of humor; I appreciate my creative ideas; I appreciate my gift with words; I appreciate my kind and gentle nature; I appreciate my curiosity and thirst for learning. After you have filled an entire page, challenge yourself to fill up yet another and even another. Then give yourself a treat and go back and read out loud every single wonderful quality you have to be thankful for and experience a surge of gratitude and well-being for just being you!

If you are experiencing negative feelings in a relationship with a child, your significant other, someone you work with, or anyone else, remembering to focus on gratitude and appreciation is an awesome tool for lifting your energy and shifting your experience of the person. Just spend a few minutes writing or even just thinking about the positive characteristics about this person in your life. Take your focus off what you don't like and consciously shift your focus onto what you do like and appreciate about this person.

You don't have to say anything to the person involved—but watch the energy shift between you. It works like magic.

You can't control anyone else's behavior but your own. Take the magnifying glass off the offending person's shortcomings; a magnifying glass makes everything look so much bigger than it really is. Pull back your focus to take in the whole picture. When we get caught up in trying to fix somebody, or feeling self-righteous about what we think they should be doing to please us, it creates a tension and friction that spirals into out-of-control negativity.

Instead, put the spotlight on what you can do to improve the situation. Aspire to shift your own behavior into a more positive place. Instead of focusing on their foibles, choose to focus on their more favorable qualities: their gifts, talents, their love for you, the caring things they do when they aren't angry or resisting you. Remember the things that used to be so attractive to you about this person? Immerse yourself in those memories. By shifting your energy in this way, very often you'll see a positive shift in how this person responds to you. If you approach them in a more loving way, they are likely to respond to you in kind. We all love to be appreciated. There is magic is expressing gratitude and appreciation. Say it out loud to a partner, a child, or a friend, and watch the person just melt as they bask in your recognition. Now that's a happy feeling place!

Yvonne came to one of my retreat programs tired of the misery that seemed to greet her every day. She was awash with anger and contempt towards her teenage daughter. She told me her daughter was making her life a "living hell." I asked Yvonne to describe her daughter to me, and what I got was an avalanche of criticism that went on for ten minutes.

When she finally stopped for air, I asked her to now describe her daughter's positive attributes. At first she couldn't think of any, as she was so caught up in her negative feelings toward her daughter. Gently, I began to ask questions, challenging her to expand her perspective and allow herself to remember the things she appreciated about her daughter. Her face softened immediately as she reconnected with her feelings of love and admiration for her daughter that had been so buried under years of disappointment and frustration. I asked her to take a moment and write these qualities down.

I asked Yvonne if she desired to improve her relationship with her daughter and, of course, she did. I suggested that she start each morning by reading this list of qualities to herself and to set her intention to look for evidence of these positive qualities each and every day. I asked her to show her appreciation for her daughter in thought, word, and action, and to strive to keep her focus on celebrating the beauty of her daughter rather than magnifying her shortcomings. The results were immediate and profound. The nasty war of words was replaced by a more peaceful co-existence. Productive communication and loving feelings began to bloom in this relationship. Yvonne felt lighter, with so much more energy, as she succeeded in shifting her focus away from what was wrong and on to what was right.

I don't mean to suggest that you should be able to transform a lifetime of negativity into joyful bliss overnight. If we could, wouldn't that be nice! But we are, after all, human beings and creatures of habit. Negativity is nothing more than a bad habit and bad habits require time, attention, and a persistent commitment to create change. If you are feeling about as far away from a joyful existence as one can imagine, then please do be patient and gentle with yourself as you strive to let go of negative feelings and open the door to a more uplifting experience of life.

There is quite a continuum of feeling states between misery and joy. Feeling angry is better than feeling depressed. At least with anger, you've got some energy to work with! A therapist once told me that depression is very often a result of anger turned inward, so finding healthy ways to express anger is indeed a good thing if you are working your way out of the depths of despair! Feeling bored is better than feeling angry; at least with boredom there is a motivation to find more excitement and stimulation in life. Feeling positive anticipation is better than feeling frustration. Hopefully you get the idea. Create an intention to move yourself progressively closer to a place where joy and contentment becomes your natural state. With time, patience, and desire, you will get there.

Another technique to assist you on your quest for *feeling good* is to close your eyes and remember a time when you felt happy. For me, a few memories that always bring me to that happy place are thinking of turning cartwheels on the beach as a young girl, lounging in a hammock with a good book, or sitting at the helm of a sailboat feeling the breeze in my hair and the salt spray in my face. What memories bring you to that joyful place? Conjure in your mind as much detail as you can, using as many senses as possible to bring the memory alive. Let the feelings of joy wash over you. Remember how it felt and how you'd like to feel now. Claim the feeling for yourself in this moment and notice how your energy soars.

The point of this exercise is to connect with the feeling experience you desire to create by ultimately achieving your dream, and to realize that, with practice, this feeling experience is available to you now. You don't have to be stuck in the cycle of "I'll be happy when..." Finding the way to feel happy right now will positively impact your quality of life! You can use this technique to go back to that happy feeling place any time you need a lift of positive energy.

Learning to live in the moment, and consciously choosing to dwell in feelings of joy, peace, and contentment, will give you the quality of life you desire right now, even as you strive to improve the circumstances of your life. The biggest thing in the way for most people is the cesspool of negativity in the form of resentment, judgment of self and others, self-pity, festering anger, and a whole host of other non-productive but pervasive debilitating feelings.

Clearing Out Negativity

In order to shift your way of being into a truly positive feeling place, you've got to do some emotional house cleaning. You may be feeling steeped in negativity about a situation in your life, and it may not be possible for you to remember in this moment how it feels to be joyful and happy. Or you may have fallen into a habit of chronic complaining and hanging on to anger and resentment so much that the idea of feeling joyful and happy seems like an unnatural act!

In either case, I recommend you do a little "burning bowl" ritual. Take out a stack of paper and write down all the negative feelings you would like to let go of to make room for more positive feelings. Be specific. Name each nuance of negative emotion you are feeling about anyone or anything in your life right now, including any negativity you direct at yourself. Begin your statements with the words *I release, I forgive,* or *I let go.* For example: I release my anger with myself for making bad choices about men in my life. I let go of my resentment toward my brother for doing better in life than I have. I forgive my father for never showing affection toward me. I let go of disappointment that my boss promoted someone else over me.

When you feel the list is complete you can do a little ceremony to let it all go. If you have a fireplace, you can burn it. If you don't have a safe place to have an actual burning ceremony, you can accomplish the same intent by tearing your papers to pieces and tossing them in the trash. Better yet, insert your paper one piece at a time into an automatic shredder machine and be uplifted by the humming sound as your negative words are sliced into tiny, unrecognizable, crumpled bits of confetti!

A word about forgiveness. This is a highly charged concept for many people. Many people refuse to consider embracing forgiveness for someone who has committed a wrong, whether perceived or real. Forgiveness is about releasing you from holding on to the pain created by the incident, not about condoning the actions or behavior of another. The damage done by hanging on to the pain and refusing to forgive others is not inflicted on the other, it is damage inflicted upon our own well-being. Release the incident to a Higher Power and get on with your life. The other party is the one who is responsible for carrying the burden of wrong-doing, not you.

Then there is the issue of forgiving ourselves. If the wrong-doer you have trouble forgiving is yourself, it is equally important to make peace with yourself. Chances are you have punished yourself relentlessly for the wrong-doing, again whether perceived or real. Now is the time to stop it. If possible, make amends, extend an olive branch, apologize, or do whatever is appropriate to assuage your guilt. Perhaps the other party is not in an emotional space to forgive. Let it go. You can only control your own choices. Pledge to yourself to live up to a higher standard of values in the future, to make choices that will do no harm to yourself and others. Accept that we are all human and that mistakes are made. Perhaps you are having trouble forgiving yourself for poor choices. Acknowledge yourself for doing the best you could at the time and move on. Strive to make better choices in the future, knowing what you know now, and applying your newfound commitment to empowering yourself.

Consciously releasing the burden of negative feelings is a powerful experience. One might even feel lost without that sense of heaviness in your gut! The truth is, all that negativity took up a great deal of energetic space and letting go of it creates a void. The opportunity now is to fill that void with positive emotion. Once you've released the negative feelings, you can now make a new list of all the wonderful positive feelings you would like to experience instead. For example: I choose to dwell in feelings of positive anticipation for the future I am creating. I choose to focus on appreciating the positive aspects of who I am, my life, my environment, and my circumstances right now. I choose love, joy, and peace. A positive, joyful experience of life is available to you right now. It is a choice that brings enormous energy and well-being to your life.

Fear, Uncertainty and Doubt

When I was working in high-tech marketing, we used to talk about the need to counter the FUD factor—Fear, Uncertainty and Doubt—with potential customers. Our strategy was to build an iron-clad case to enable our customers to view a potential purchase of our products and services with confidence and positive expectation. In other words, the job of our sales and marketing folks was to shift our customer's mindset from one of negative thought and feeling to one of positive thought and feeling about doing business with us. It always feels better to make a decision in the absence of fear, uncertainty, and doubt, or at least when those fears and anxieties are held at bay with a more powerful, overriding vision of a positive outcome.

We all have fears, uncertainty, and doubt about decisions, circumstances, and outcomes in our lives. I would be highly suspect of anyone who tried to tell me otherwise. The difference between living a life that's a struggle and a life that flows with ease is whether you allow those fears and anxieties to rule the day, or whether you make a choice to focus on creating your desired experiences and outcomes. The difference is where you put your energy. It is a conscious choice to dwell in positive thought and feeling and a choice that results in abundant rewards.

Sometimes feelings of fear, uncertainty, and doubt are exacerbated by the need to be in total control. I know it is easier said than done, but let it go. Let go of the need to be in control. This may sound incongruent with the idea that you can create the future you desire by visualizing what you want in detail. It is not. Think of it as putting a stake in the ground. Being intentional about what you want and how you want it to unfold is an important step on the journey, as you will see in Stepping Stone Five. However, it is equally important to let go of your attachment to the precise outcome, meaning the how, the when, or in what form your desires manifest. In other words, be prepared to go with the flow. Often times, we can't even imagine the extent of what is possible and what we think of in our limited minds as the ideal scenario may, in fact, pale to what actually shows up.

How Coaching Found Me

In the summer of 2000, six months into my new life as a marketing consultant, I was browsing in Barnes and Noble when a book nearly flew off the shelf into my arms. It was Cheryl Richardson's *Take Time For Your Life, A Personal Coach's 7-Step Program for Creating the Life You Want*. I was riveted on the words Personal Coach. I had heard of this profession about a year earlier and was intrigued and excited, but I had told myself at the time that it was a pipe dream for me to think of making a career change that dramatic! I had over fifteen years invested in my high-tech marketing career. By now, I had dealt with a lot of my fears and was much more open to the possibility of change in a new direction. My intuition kicked into high gear and I heard it calling! I bought the book and took it home with me.

I absorbed this book cover to cover and felt a growing excitement I could not contain. "I want to be the next Cheryl Richardson," I thought. "How can I learn to be a coach?" I flipped to the back of the book and found references to the International Coach Federation and immediately embarked on an impassioned quest for knowledge. I interviewed the three coaching schools that were accredited at the time, and chose the best fit for me, The Academy for Coach Training (ACT) in Seattle. I had spoken with the two other coaching schools, but when I spoke to the founder of ACT, I knew she was someone special. She exuded warmth, sincerity, and a spiritual magnetism that drew me in and embraced me. I signed up right away for the first class in the coach-training curriculum.

My timing was perfect—the next training series was beginning in three weeks and not only that, the first two classes were being offered in Southern California. YES! My consulting work made it possible for me to have the flexibility and the finances to take off for a week at a time to attend these trainings.

It was love at first sight! Though I felt apprehensive when, right off the bat, we were asked to do practice coaching sessions with other classmates. Once I got past the fear of being inept, I discovered I had a natural gift for being a coach. The skills came naturally to me. I supposed in some ways, I had been coaching people all my life. I felt like at long last I had found my calling. I absolutely loved it! I couldn't get enough of it. I signed up for the full certification process at a fast-track pace. I was ready and eager to do the work. What I wasn't prepared for was the absolutely magical experience that awaited me. I hadn't known specifically what my future was going to look like in terms of the job or career that would make my heart sing. By focusing on how I wanted to feel, and finding joy in the journey, the answer found me.

Life is truly an adventure. Who knows what lies under the next stone or behind door number three? You may discover something that opens new avenues of possibility. If your best-laid plans seem to come up short at times, or you feel like maybe you are barking up the wrong tree, be alert to the message in what might seem a failure or a detour in the moment. Let go of the need to be in control and be open to opportunities and outcomes that may surprise you. Keep a positive attitude and approach to your endeavors and strive to stay in a place of positive feeling. Shift from an expectation of "I'll be happy when..." to a reality of "I am happy now and joyfully anticipating each new day, each new opportunity, and a world of possibility!"

In Stepping Stone Five we will build on the art of positive thought and feeling by combining it with the conscious use of imagination. You will learn how to create a compelling personal vision statement that will serve as your beacon of light to guide you forward into a future of your own design!

Part III:
Bringing Your Dreams Into Reality

"Cherish your visions and your dreams as they are the children of your soul; the blueprints of your future accomplishments."

–Napoleon Hill

◆ Stepping Stone Five:

Creating a Compelling Personal Vision
Imagining you are already where you want to be

Vision is the art of seeing clearly
what lies in your heart.

Through my work as a life coach, I've become almost evangelical regarding the value of having a clear and compelling personal vision for your life. I believe all seven of the stepping stones on the journey are extremely important, but if I had to identify only one and give up the other six, I'd have to choose this one as the most indispensable. There is something about having a really exciting personal vision that will propel you forward with great momentum. The joy in the vision is so great it tends to overpower any self-doubt or self-sabotaging tendencies that get in the way!

Having a compelling and positive vision for the future is vital in order to feel energized and upbeat in the face of challenging or less than ideal circumstances. Studies show there is a correlation between being depressed and perceiving that you have no control over your destiny. When you are feeling down, you are likely to feel cut off from hope and possibility and devoid of a vision for a better future. I have seen it over and over again with my clients. Once we have reached a point where we are able to craft a vision statement that makes their eyes light up, their feelings of discouragement, of being lost and afraid, and of hopelessness just melt away.

A powerful vision is a product of the imagination. It's a result of being able to look into the future, past apparent obstacles and limitations in the present, to see your ultimate, glorious, desired destination. Whoa! That's a mouthful. It's not easy either, or most of us would not have a need for this book! In this chapter, we will look at ways you can play in your imagination and how to harness its power to clarify your personal vision for your life.

The Power of the Imagination

I'm in awe of my seventeen-year-old son when it comes to his vivid and extraordinary imagination. When he was just eighteen months old, he was playing happily with a set of Duplos, the toddler version of Legos building blocks. Suddenly, he seemed to get an inspiration and his hands moved rapidly grabbing a series of pieces and chunking them together.

In a flash of activity, he completed his masterpiece and turned to look at me with his creation held proudly in his outstretched arms. He said, "Ma Ma, Toot!" My jaw dropped. My baby had just created a very realistic rendition of a choo-choo train engine complete with wheels and a smokestack. That's not in the expected skill set of a year-and-a-half-old child!

As my son grew, this talent for visualizing would reveal itself in his drawings. Military tanks, airplanes, fancy racecars, and robots all drawn in intricate detail with views from the side, from the front, from the rear—and from the top and bottom as well. I was absolutely amazed at his ability to imagine things with such clarity and from so many angles. My son is truly gifted with extraordinary imagination.

I've seen how my son creates what he wants in life. His first car is the product of his vivid imagination and unyielding belief that if he could picture it, he could have it. He manifested the job he wanted by imagining it. This child has always had wisdom beyond his years. He really gets the power of positive thinking and has an innate understanding of the power of visualization. I can't wait to see how these talents play out in a career pursuit for him!

My son apparently got these spatial thinking genes from his father, because I can't even comprehend being able to rotate things in my head and see images of such detail. I have had difficulty in my life trying to visualize things in my head. I have attempted guided visualizations in many different settings over the years, usually coming away totally frustrated with the experience. I get wispy images at best while the person sitting next to me might get a full Technicolor movie. I had drawn the conclusion that I simply lacked imagination!

What puzzled me, though, is that when it came to fearful imaginings I was a master at visualizing disaster scenarios. You know, if I hadn't heard from my husband by the expected hour, I was sure the plane had crashed. When I was in high school, starring in the school plays, that's when I would experience vivid imaginings of every possible thing that could go wrong: showing up late, forgetting my lines, falling flat on my face in center stage, or stepping on the hem of my skirt resulting in an embarrassing wardrobe malfunction! But for some reason, using the power of imagination to visualize perfect, highly desirable, magnificent outcomes eluded me. Instead, I was plagued with unwanted visions of disaster.

There is incredible power in the imagination. Power that is often wasted on worries and worst-case scenarios. It is so easy when times are tough to spend an inordinate amount of time and mental energy worrying about what you don't want, what you fear, and creating elaborate game plans to deal with all the things that could go wrong. All this does is perpetuate and deepen feelings of anxiety. What if you could channel all that energy into visualizing what you do want?! First of all, it feels a whole lot better than worry, and it creates a positive state of being that propels you toward the outcomes that you do want.

Learning to Visualize Effectively

I was much relieved to discover that it is possible to harness the imagination in multiple ways, which don't all have to look like Technicolor movies in your head! Some people are primarily visual in that they gather information about the world around them through what they see, so it follows that mental visualization would be easy and effortless for them. Others of us are more kinesthetic, gathering information through touch and physical experience. Some of us are auditory, absorbing the greatest amount of information through what we hear. Some of us are intuitive and have a sixth sense that allows us to gather information through a certain kind of feeling or inner knowing. We are all so very different, so it is important to honor your personal style when embarking on a mission to harness the power of your imagination!

I encourage you to acknowledge your personal brand of sensory awareness and to consciously employ your favored senses to vividly imagine what you want in your life. Along the path of my own journey I have learned that there are three very powerful methods of visualizing that will enable you to breathe life into your ideas, hopes, and dreams for your future. The first is working with images, which can either be held in your mind or expressed through a collection of physical pictures. The second is working with the written word through journaling, which can be free flowing or highly structured. The third approach is working with the spoken word, which can be accomplished alone, for your ears only, or by using a trusted friend or professional coach to be your sounding board. I recommend experimenting with all three methods and ultimately using any one or all three methods as they suit your style. Regardless of what method you use to get there, having a crystal-clear vision helps you move toward a future that is brighter and more empowering. We will now look at all three of these methods of imagining in detail.

Working With Visual Images

As you start to work with your imagination, I encourage you to indulge in some good old-fashioned daydreaming about the future you want to create. Find some quiet time for yourself in a place where you will not be disturbed or distracted. Just allow yourself to play in your mind for a while and notice what images or impressions, however fleeting, begin to appear. Please suspend the need to judge or be practical and just see what shows up for you. Keep a journal handy and start recording these ideas and images as they occur.

Ideally, you would employ all the senses. Imagine not only seeing what it looks like, but what does it *feel* like when you have it? Are you content, joyful or positively exuberant? Can you smell the environment—perhaps the ocean air or the scent of flowers or trees in your garden? Can you imagine the sleek feel of the hood of your brand-new convertible as you run your hand across it or feel yourself sink into the leather seats as you sit behind the wheel? Can you hear the sound of the surf outside your home or the applause from the audience as you stand on stage? Can you taste the champagne as you toast your success or the sweetness of the wedding cake on your tongue as you celebrate having a new life partner?

For some this activity will be easy and fun, for others it might feel baffling, frustrating, or downright frivolous. If you have trouble visualizing, just let go of high expectations and work with whatever wispy images or impressions that you do get and trust that they are significant. If you are blessed with a vivid imagination I invite you to employ it to the fullest! Contrary to what your parents or teachers used to say, daydreaming can be quite productive if you use it as a conscious tool to create a desirable vision for your future.

After spending time working with mental images, you can bring even more clarity and focus to your vision by working with physical pictures. I discovered the power of this technique while attending my Artist's Way workshop. One of the assignments in this class was to create a collage of images that represented what we loved most and what we wanted to create in our future. I set about the task of collecting pictures and words from magazines that energized me and represented my desires.

We were asked to spend only twenty minutes or so putting together the actual arrangement of pictures on our poster board. Not me. Something powerful came over me as I sat down with these images. I played for hours, like a child with a new art project. Totally out of character for myself, I stayed up until 1:00 in the morning two nights in a row, arranging my pictures until I had a masterpiece. It came together like a stained glass window, colorful and multifaceted with each picture blending into the next, telling a magnificent story. It was beautiful. And it was me.

I still remember the incredible joy I felt in expressing myself this way, in being able to visually see all that I desired to create in my life. And I felt a wonderful sense of possibility and empowerment as I surveyed my finished collage. I still have this collage hanging in my office and I can say that I have fully lived into this vision I created years ago. A collage like this serves as a visual statement of intention, an ever-present reminder of what is important to you and where you are going in life.

Try your hand at creating a picture collage of your own. You can use poster board or a scrapbook. You can cover every inch or leave a lot of white space. Organize it randomly or in categories. Use words and pictures you cut from a magazine, greeting cards, and photographs, or draw your own pictures and illustrate with calligraphy. Do whatever pleases you. This is an expression of who you are and where you are going. Make it as unique as you are. Have fun with this and remember the only limits are the ones you allow. So let go of the shackles that bind you and play!

Let yourself imagine having it all, all that you have ever wanted and make an extraordinary visual statement about the future that you intend to step into. It is a path of your choosing. It does not matter where you are today. Focus your attention and your desire on where you want to go and over time, you will see how the path opens up for you to get there.

There is one caveat. Treat these pictures as literal requests. It's the old adage—be careful what you ask for—you just might get it! Be very specific about what you desire in your picture collage. If you want to have a baby, don't put a picture of an empty baby carriage in your collage! Make sure there is an actual baby pictured in the carriage! Also, some people want to approach this project as a representation of before and after. If you are feeling stuck or unhappy with your current circumstances, don't spend an ounce of energy putting pictures together that represent the status quo. Keep the focus and all your energy on crafting a masterpiece that represents where you want to be, not where you have been! Your collage will be more powerful and effective for you as a representation of where you are going—a future you can step into.

I have one more example of what not to do from my own experience. I chose the word "Potential" in big letters and put it at the top of my collage. That's nice…but I later realized having great potential was not my goal! Having potential and actually manifesting your dreams are worlds apart. I eventually replaced that word with the words "Make a Difference."

Another visual method of fueling the imagination that would appeal to both visual and kinesthetic types is to employ a process called Feng Shui. This is an ancient art used to set up your physical environment in specific ways to represent the things you desire to manifest in your life. Your home is divided into areas representing the important aspects of your life, including career, relationships, children, health, and more. So, for example, in the relationship corner of your house, you might want to place a painting that elicits the feeling of a happy relationship for you. I'm not a Feng Shui expert and I know I am greatly oversimplifying how it works. I find it a fun and inspiring way to create visual and tactile reminders of the things I want to achieve in my life. There are many books and consultants available if this is an idea you'd like to explore.

Write it Down!

I am a huge proponent of using a personal journal to capture thoughts, feelings, ideas, challenges, and opportunities. Writing really works for me. Writing things out helps me immensely to process my feelings and to get my arms around a challenge or difficult situation. I believe much of my own personal growth has been as a result of my prolific relationship with my journal! Writing brings my experiences alive and writing adds a sense of realism to what might otherwise seem a fantasy. Writing down dreams brings them a significant step closer to reality. A journal is for your eyes only and is a wonderful place to let your imagination soar and to allow dreams to blossom.

Writing in your journal is a fabulous way to exercise your imagination using word pictures. A journal is a place for free-flowing thoughts and feelings. This is not a place to be concerned about using perfect grammar or complete sentences. Forget about hanging participles! Nor is it a place to be concerned about neatness. Just get the thoughts out. I highly encourage you to treat yourself to a lovely bound journal, one whose design gives you pleasure and makes you want to curl up with it for a while.

I will confess, however, that when I first started serious journaling, I had such a deeply ingrained perfectionist streak, that I couldn't get started in a pretty journal. I was afraid I would mess it up! I found the only way I could really let go in a journal was to buy an inexpensive spiral bound notebook like kids use in school. That way I could scribble and cross out to my heart's content and not judge myself for it. I have stacks of these flimsy little notebooks in my closet filled to the brim with the odyssey of my life! Somewhere along the line, I let go of that worry about messing up a nice journal and finally gave myself the gift of a beautiful hardbound journal. Now I have stacks of those in the closet too. Choose whatever will work for you and get started!

The most effective way to use your journal as a tool to imagine your future is to focus on what you want, not what you don't want. However, if you are stuck, let yourself journal profusely about all the things that aren't working for you until you get it out of your system. For some this could take hours, days, or even weeks. Do this with the intention that once you've spilled out all the negativity you can muster, that you will shift your focus to thinking about and imagining what you do want to have in your life instead.

When you're all done with your diatribe about what you don't want, I want you to get a brand new journal and start to work on putting into words, *passionate words,* what it is you do want. Write about your ideal life in as much detail and using as many sensing words as possible. You want to feel what it's like to be living your new life. When you imagine this new life, do you feel joyful, exuberant, excited, and energetic? Write about how it feels for you as you visualize your new life. If you are not feeling it yet, write about how you imagine you will feel when you are living your dream.

As you begin to imagine your ideal life, it is important to think about all aspects of your life. The focus of your dream may be creating a new career direction or attracting a certain amount of income. Don't forget to include the things in your vision that create balance and the quality of life you desire. Think about all of the following categories when imagining the life you want to have:

Career/Business

Physical Body/Health

Play/Enjoyment

Lifestyle

Creative Expression/Hobbies

Love Relationship/Life Partner

Children/Family

Extended Family

Friends

Pets

Spirituality/Religion

Emotional Well-being

Personal Growth/Learning

Home Environment

Travel/Vacations

Prosperity/Wealth

Fame/Recognition

Service/Contribution

Anything else that is important to you!

Be sure to write about your desires for your life in each of these areas and you will be on your way to a balanced and joyful life! If you aren't big on writing prose, then make a series of lists describing what you want in each area in as much detail as you can muster.

If you do have a creative flair for writing, try your hand at writing a movie script with you as the star. Create a script for your new life. Start with "A Day in the Life" and expand from there. If, for example, one of your desires is to find a life partner, write a story that reveals the qualities of the person you imagine being your partner, how he makes you feel, the way you spend time together, the values you share. Pick an important occasion such as your birthday, anniversary, or religious holiday and write a story about how you spend the day together. Just have fun with the writing and let your journal house a wealth of ideas and word images that create a compelling vision for you to live into.

If a free-flowing, creative approach to writing is daunting, overwhelming, or even a bit too airy-fairy for you, try using a more structured approach. A writing structure helps if you are someone who is more analytical and have a need to approach things in a way that feels more practical to you. One structure you can use that will help you focus specifically on imagining your desired future, is to work with these three questions:

> What do I want?
>
> Why do I want it?
>
> Why do I believe I can be, do, or have it?

You can do this for one grand, overarching desire or you can use this structure over and over again, focusing in on one particular desire at a time.

Choose the approach that feels the most appealing to you. I encourage everyone to give a try to all these approaches to journaling, to experiment and play until you find the method that suits you best. Journaling is a tool you can use every day of your life. If it feels good to you, do it!

Say it Out Loud!

There is power in hearing yourself declare your desires for your future out loud. Until you are feeling rock solid about your direction, I would advise being careful about who you choose to reveal your thoughts to. You don't want to subject yourself to an onslaught from the doubters choir! Take inventory of the people around you and determine who you can trust to listen without judgment or projecting their worries and doubts onto you. This is where a life coach can be truly invaluable as well. It is important to find someone who can be a sounding board for your ideas, hold the vision with you, and support your efforts to move in the direction to fulfill your dreams.

If there isn't anyone you feel comfortable sharing your vision with, find a place you can be in solitude and declare your desires out loud. For example, you might say "I am in a loving relationship with my life partner, who cherishes me as I cherish him," or "I see my best-selling children's books on display at Borders." Speak with passion and conviction and allow the universe to be your witness. Remember it is always more powerful to speak as if your dream is already here.

If the statement you say out loud leaves you feeling flat, then work at it until you find just the right words that will excite you and ignite your energy. If you can't find words that excite you, then my guess would be that you are working from a place of "I should want this" rather than from a place of "I deeply desire this for my life." If this is the case, go back to Stepping Stones Two and Three to work through some of your blocks to allowing yourself to have what you want!

Connecting With the Essence of Who You Are

The purpose of the Stepping Stones, so far, has been to give you a flexible structure and a thought-provoking process for building a better relationship with yourself. In doing so, you have in a sense put your needs, desires, dreams, and feelings under a microscope to gain an understanding of what you are truly about, what makes you tick, and what makes your heart sing. You've also spent time creating a more positive inner environment that will enable your dreams to flourish.

As a result, a clearer image of *you* is emerging. You are now more connected to the combination of positive qualities that make you uniquely you. In the past, you may have allowed your focus to dwell on "what's wrong with me" instead of "what's right with me!" Joyfully moving forward in life and giving wings to your dreams happens when you are able to fully and completely embrace the wonderful woman that you are. Acknowledging what makes you special, what your hidden treasures are, and bringing them to the forefront, with confidence, energy, and focus, will propel you to incredible achievements. That's why a personal vision statement is so powerful. It's an acknowledgment of who you are at the deepest level, the gifts you have to offer in life, and your heartfelt sense of purpose.

If you have spent any time in a corporate environment, you would likely be familiar with the idea of a company or department mission statement. These are statements that express the way the company sees itself in the marketplace and how it wishes its customers to view its products and services. It becomes the yardstick by which courses of action are evaluated and decisions are reached.

I had done mission statements for over fifteen years in my high-tech career. It was not until I embarked on my path to become a life coach that I had ever come across the concept of a personal vision statement. This was a novel idea to me—an idea I embraced with curiosity and an open mind. In doing so, I discovered one of the keys to creating quality of life!

A personal vision statement is a succinct yet colorful statement that captures your highest aspiration for how you see yourself in the world, combined with your sense of purpose for your life. An effective vision statement expresses this with feeling words that deeply energize you. It is a statement that is a reflection of your values and the essence of who you are.

Mid-way through my training curriculum to become a certified professional coach, I was required to take an intensive workshop designed to lead each of us to a deeper self-awareness and understanding. For a full day, we focused on excavating clues about the qualities that represented our essence and the characteristics that made us each unique. We explored the passions and values that we held dear. The culmination of the day yielded a work of art as far as I was concerned: my personal vision statement in words that made my heart sing.

As I stood before the group and recited my masterpiece, I was overcome with emotion. I felt wave after wave of goose bumps flowing over me, tears welling in my eyes. I had never felt so seen, so understood, so validated in all my life. I felt seen at the level of my soul and truly, deeply and lovingly embraced for who I was at the deepest level. This was me! My personal vision statement captured my spirit and I felt as if I had sprouted golden wings and could take flight.

Here is the vision statement I created that day:

> I am a passionate dreamer. Insightful, multifaceted, vibrant, colorful, courageous, and grounded; following my intuition on golden wings and connected with jubilance to my spiritual center. My purpose is to artfully inspire, to see possibilities and to give wings to dreams.

I was totally enthralled by this process. I left the workshop with a deeper commitment and an unshakable inner knowing that I was moving my life in the right direction. The seed for this book, *Give Wings To Your Dreams,* though I didn't know it at the time, was planted that day!

Helping my clients to create their personal vision statements has become the centerpiece of my coaching practice. Working the stepping stones creates a foundation of self-acceptance and well-being, a deeper understanding of personal needs, desires and dreams, and a nurturing inner environment conducive to beginning work on this important milestone.

There is something magical about the process of creating this very personal vision statement and the power it has to propel clients forward with newfound confidence, excitement, and conviction. I'll share a few of my clients' vision statements. You'll notice that they are unique and varied. What they have in common is that each statement crackles with energy for the individual who crafted it. To each of them, it represents a beautiful mirror, a reflection of the beauty that they are and the passions they hold dear. Before sharing their statements, I'll tell you a little about who they are.

Prior to working with me, Jackie had spent a great deal of the previous nine months in bed. She was working with a therapist to conquer the deep despair and depression that had set in after her painful and ugly divorce left her emotionally devastated. She had been married for over twenty years. She was self-employed and had been unable to go through the motions of showing up for work. Her life was a shambles and she was very, very unhappy. After working the process of the Seven Stepping Stones, she had regained her vitality and her belief in herself. We spent an intensive retreat day together to craft her personal vision statement:

> I am a proud and powerful woman in the sunrise of my life. I embrace each new horizon with gratitude and grace. I am motivated, capable, creative, and clearly focused. My purpose is to achieve unconditional love and acceptance, and to allow myself, and others, to blossom with strength, love and beauty.

Two years later Jackie was excited to report that her business was thriving, actually double her previous best year, and she was in a new love relationship that was heading toward commitment. She had remodeled her house and deepened her relationship with her family. She has totally embraced her vision.

Eva had reached a point of profound burnout. She was working such long hours that she had practically moved into her employer's office! She was mentally, emotionally and physically exhausted. Her facial expression had molded into a permanent frown. After working the Seven Stepping Stones with me, she had regained a sense of balance and enough energy to begin to see new possibilities for her life. After a few months of telephone coaching sessions, we spent an intensive retreat day together to craft her personal vision statement:

> I am a stunning, vivacious, passionate, and talented woman—full of vibrant energy and love, with a boundless intellect, a wicked wit, and joie de vivre. I am balanced, calm, and free. My purpose is to extract the honey of life; to explore and celebrate divine romance, intricate mysteries, sensual pleasures and lyrical delights; to create beauty with signature style and grace.

Eva left that day the total embodiment of her vision, positively buzzing with energy, and a joyful anticipation to get back home and experience life from this new perspective. She has since created a life full of fun, laughter, and creative pursuits. She's no longer a workaholic; she now places a high value on taking care of herself and making time for the things that give her life a sense of balance and wholeness.

Patrice was at a crossroad and looking for direction in her life. Her divorce from her husband of nine years had ended without a lot of drama, but she still held on to a great deal of anger and resentment. She had chronic health issues that limited her choices. She had been going to work and coming home to crash for a very long time. She was completely out of touch with the things that would bring her joy in life and felt like she was starting over with a blank sheet of paper. She had a long and successful career in a technical sales field, but she was feeling bored with it. She wanted a new job or career direction that would give her more intellectual stimulation, but wanted to be careful not to take on something that would create even more imbalance in her life. She exuded the weight of the world on her shoulders and a pervasive sadness when we first met. She was drawn to the idea of a retreat getaway to rethink her life. At the end of our first day together, this is the vision and purpose statement that emerged for her:

> I am content, peaceful, vibrant and happy; Intellectually stimulated, playfully inspired and fulfilled; an independent, confident, goal-oriented woman; Deeply gratified through loving, intimate relationships and nurtured by aesthetically pleasing surroundings. My purpose is to embrace and enjoy the adventure of lifelong learning for personal and intellectual growth.

She left with a commitment to pursue more pleasurable activities in order to create more balance in her life and to let go of her anger with her ex-husband and get on with creating her own full and satisfying life. Less than a week after she returned home from the retreat, she was offered a new position with her company that played to all her strengths and knowledge, maintained the level of freedom and reasonable hours she'd become accustomed to in sales, yet offered her new and exciting intellectual challenges. She was delighted!

It is amazing how quickly life begins to change for the better once you make a profound shift in perspective by focusing on a positive and energizing vision of who you are and what you would like to experience in your life!

Crafting Your Personal Vision Statement

Now that you've been through the Stepping Stone process, you can create your own compelling vision statement. Go back and read what you've written in your journal and look at the picture collage you have created. From these two sources, begin to build a list of words and phrases that represent exciting aspects of who you are and who you are becoming; words that describe what you love and what you value deeply; words that describe what you desire and what you aspire to do with your life. Challenge yourself to fill an entire page with these descriptive words. You'll be amazed at how many wonderful words tell the story of who you are and what is important to you. Once you have a robust list in front of you, take a few moments to enjoy the energy collected on this piece of paper. Revel in the realization that you are all of these things and so much more.

Now, it gets a bit more challenging. From this long and beautiful list of words, circle the ten or twenty that are the most exciting and energizing to you. Try not to think about it too much, just go for the words that jump off the paper at you. Next write the words you've circled on a new sheet of paper. These are the primary words and phrases you'll want to use to craft your vision statement. You want to capture the essence of who you are and what you desire in a succinct two or three sentence statement that starts with the words, "I am." Add feeling words to give it more juice.

Once you've created your "I am" statement, create a sentence that starts with the words, "My purpose is..." The "I am" statement describes who you are. The purpose statement will capture what is important for you to do in the world. The clues are revealed in your list of words and phrases. Draw out the ones that have energy for you. Look back at the examples if you get stuck. Remember, this does not have to be a lofty statement about being the one to create world peace. It's a statement that reflects what will bring you the quality of life that will make your heart sing!

Take your time with this process and don't expect to make your masterpiece the first time you string some words together. Keep playing with it, tweaking it. If you are doing it right, you'll have a page full of scratch outs and scribbles. It's a messy process! Keep at it until you can say, "Yes!" with gusto. You want to be able read this statement and feel a profound connection and knowing that "This is who I am! This is my purpose!" You'll know you've got a great statement when reading it gives you an energy boost, maybe even goose bumps!

Once you have crafted your vision and purpose, read this statement several times a day, particularly first thing in the morning and at night before you go to bed. With clarity of vision and persistence in keeping your vision present in your heart and mind, you will find that you just naturally begin to move productively in the direction of your dream.

On A Clear Day, You Can See Forever

The tools we have talked about so far in this chapter will help you to start bringing your dreams into crystal-clear focus and to create a vision that holds power and excitement for you. Having a clear vision gives you a greater sense of meaning and purpose as you go through your day-to-day life. A clear vision creates focus and momentum. And a clear vision gives you a wonderful sense of hope and possibility. A clear vision opens up a pathway for you to begin your journey into a future of your own creation. Are you feeling excited yet? Having a powerful vision is a cause to celebrate!

Now that you have created your powerful vision statement, everything else from this point forward will become easier, because now you have a beacon of light to guide you on your life path. A ship that sets sail for a distant shore needs a map to guide its path. In Stepping Stone Six we will look at creating a life plan that will serve as your roadmap to get you from where you are now, to where you want to go.

Harnessing the Power of Intention

Creating an inspiring life plan

> *"Without leaps of imagination, or dreaming,*
> *we lose the excitement of possibilities.*
> *Dreaming after all, is a form of planning."*
>
> –Gloria Steinem

Your personal vision is a treasure to behold! It is the overarching statement that sets the context for your life going forward. Coupled with an inspiring life plan, it becomes a powerful lightning rod, attracting positive energy, people, and circumstances into your life. It becomes the yardstick by which you measure any course of action, any decision, or any choice that you will make on your life's journey.

Your personal vision gives you great clarity. Clarity is like the sun breaking through on a cloudy day, illuminating possibilities that have been previously obscured from view. Armed with an energizing personal vision, you now have a clear mental image of the quality of life you desire. And like any navigator, you will need to outfit yourself with a really good map to chart your course between where you are now and where you want to go. Like a trusty compass, a well-thought-out life plan will set your course and keep you moving in your desired direction.

Ready. Fire. Aim.

In the frenetic world of Silicon Valley, we used to jokingly say, "Ready. Fire. Aim." We were poking fun at the chaotic way we tried to move forward when the pace was so fast nobody had time to plan. You can get away with it for a while, but sooner or later it catches up with you. Decisions are made in a vacuum, scattered efforts dilute resources and expensive mistakes are made. Anyone can tell you that conducting a business without a plan is a recipe for eventual failure. Yet most of us conduct our *lives* without having a plan.

Ready. Fire. Aim. It seems to be a fitting description for how we tend to approach life. We go where the commotion is, where the demands are placed upon us, where the momentum takes us, without any conscious decisions on our part. In the absence of a deliberate plan and a clear set of intentions for how we wish to conduct our life, is it any wonder we wind up adrift in a life that isn't working for us? If we are ever to achieve a quality of life that pleases us, we have to take time out to create a plan that will serve as our roadmap to guide us on the journey toward our destination.

Getting Intentional

I reached the age of forty-three before being exposed to the concept of having a written plan for my life. After creating my personal vision statement during my coach training class in Seattle, I was introduced to a powerful process for life planning. I went home and completed my comprehensive life plan detailing the intentions

I had for all the important aspects of my life, along with specific choices and actions I would commit to in support of my intentions. I'll share a few excerpts from the life plan I created for myself, just as I was beginning to see clearly what I wanted for my life.

My intention for my career was:

> I am magically transitioning into work that makes my heart sing and makes a difference in the quality of life for people.

I think I chose the word "magically" at the time, because I didn't know exactly how I was going to transition into such a radically different career. I only knew I wanted very passionately to find a way. I was ready to take a leap of faith because I knew from the depths of my soul that I was meant to do work that would inspire people to embrace positive change.

The next step, designed to add a more concrete dimension to my life plan, was to articulate a series of choices I would make to breathe even more life into my intention. In other words, I created choice statements that would guide my decisions to take specific actions over the next several months to a year. My choices to support my intention for my career were:

> Become a certified professional coach
>
> Offer coaching services on a part-time basis immediately
>
> Establish a full-time coaching business within two years
>
> Take baby steps toward becoming an inspirational public speaker

> Open my heart and awareness to synchronistic events
>
> Be willing to take risks to make it happen

With these choices clearly articulated, I then made a list of actions I was committed to take that would move me forward. Here are a few of those actions.

My commitment to action:

> Complete my full certification-training program with ACT by November 2001
>
> Obtain ICF certification within two years
>
> Establish a business and create basic marketing materials within 60 days
>
> Contact friends, associates, and acquaintances to announce my coaching practice
>
> Develop a speech and speak for free for local women's groups
>
> Listen to my intuition and follow the guidance
>
> Journal daily and visualize my success!

Looking back, I am truly in awe of the power of intention. Taking the time to create a written plan to capture everything you desire for your life, along with a game plan for how to achieve it creates amazing results. My life plan included intention statements, choices and actions for all aspects of my life that I wanted to bring energy and attention to. Here are a couple more of the intention statements I created in my life plan.

My intention for my home environment was:

> I am living where the air is crisp and clean with ocean breeze, joyfully settled in a home that is full of natural light, bright with pleasing color, and spaciously meeting my family's every need.

At the time I wrote the above intention, I was living in the midst of the stress and congestion of Silicon Valley. I had a long-held dream of living in an ocean community with a home close enough to take daily walks on the beach. I had been fantasizing about moving to San Diego for some time, and had taken a vacation with my kids the previous summer to check out the town and the high-tech market there. Along the way, driving along the coast highway, we passed through Santa Barbara, a town that calls itself the American Riviera. I fell in love! I thought to myself, "If only I could find a way to live here!"

My intention for creativity in my life was:

> I am creatively birthing inspirational writing with ease.

This one showed up as a bit of a surprise to me. I had not written anything to speak of, other than reports, plans, and proposals in a corporate setting, and some heartfelt poetry in my private journal. The self-discovery process I embarked on during my coach training program had reconnected me with my long-time desire to write a book that would help women like me, or at least to publish helpful articles in women's magazines. I hadn't ever attempted it, other than making some sketchy notes, because I didn't know how, and I didn't really believe I could. Caught up in the inspiration and the energy of the process, I thought, "Why not think big? You never know!"

When you get intentional about your life, it's best to strap on your seatbelt, as things begin to happen really fast. In my case, it happened so fast it made my head spin. The sequence of events that moved me forward was not what I would have choreographed; you know: something safe and sensible. They were in fact, rather intense!

Taking a Leap of Faith

I created my life plan in December 2000, and what incredibly fortunate timing it turned out to be. Two months later, the bottom dropped out of the job market in Silicon Valley and I got caught up in the massive layoffs. Consultants were among the first to go.

I was approaching my one-year anniversary of consulting with the same company, and had every reason to expect my contract to be renewed for yet another year. Suddenly, with only two weeks' notice, I was out of work. The president of the agency called me personally to say "Lauren, the situation is grim, we have no other job prospects for you and I suggest you call everyone you know in Silicon Valley… and beg!"

My first reaction was panic and horror and to succumb to my inner-gremlin voice bashing me, "See I told you, you shouldn't have left your salaried job!" (Not that my salaried job would have been any safer, but at least a layoff would have come with a nice severance package.) I found myself in my worst-case scenario, out on my butt with no income and no job prospects in sight. And the gremlin had a field day: "What kind of mother are you, taking this kind of risk—you have children to feed!"

I was facing a crossroad. After about 24 hours of panic and tears, a light came on and I made a powerful choice. I felt I had been sent a very clear message from the universe, a sort of cosmic kick in the pants, launching me more quickly than I had planned down the path of my new vision and purpose.

You see, I had it all figured out. I was going to very sensibly, gradually, and gracefully reduce my hours doing marketing consulting and increase my hours doing my new coaching work and everything would be safe. My vision of an ideal transition was not to be. This is where not being attached to the details of a particular outcome really comes in handy.

Rather than seeing the layoff as something to be devastated about, I began to see it as something to rejoice about. It opened the way for me to move very quickly in the direction of my passion. In fact, I got my "magical transition."

Intentional living opens you to a powerful experience of synchronicity—being in the right place at the right time, meeting helpful people who lead you to just the right resource, and finding opportunities that just seem to fall in your lap. I found myself totally in the flow. I made a series of huge decisions guided by faith that my vision and purpose for my life was right, and that there was no better time than the present to go for it.

Santa Barbara, Here I Come!

It looked as if the real estate market in Silicon Valley was going to take a deep dive soon and I decided to put my house on the market and cash out. My intention was to use some of the money to invest in building my business. My oldest son would be entering high school in the next school year and I wanted to make a life-style change and get my kids out of the pressure cooker environment. I felt this was the best window of opportunity I was going to get. My sister had just moved from Los Angeles to Santa Barbara, adding fuel to my desire to live there. My boyfriend did the kind of work where he had the option to either telecommute or work as an independent consultant, so it seemed like it could work for us. With some reticence, he agreed to go on this adventure with me, and move to Santa Barbara, though we decided I would go first, and he would join me after I got settled in.

My real estate agent told me to expect my house to sit on the market for a while, as things were not moving like they used to. Yet, my house sold in the first weekend on the market. Not only that, it sold at full price, in as is condition, and with the proviso that we got to stay in the house until the end of the school year. It was perfect! My agent's jaw dropped in amazement.

I decided to look for a house to rent in Santa Barbara, rather than invest in a new house right away. The real estate conditions were quite different there. I was told repeatedly that rentals were nearly impossible to get, that I'd be competing with at least twenty other highly qualified applicants, and that finding something nice was hopeless. Yet, in a single weekend trip, I found a lovely home in a great family neighborhood with the very best schools and a peaceful backyard garden. I secured a rental agreement within the week. The locals said, "How did you do that?!" It just felt so meant to be and I was feeling unstoppable.

Just over a year later, a client who I had coached through a career transition from computer sales to real estate sales called to say she had found the perfect home for my boys and me and she was right. The minute I walked into this house, I knew I had to have it, and so I bought my Santa Barbara home. It was right there in my life plan in my intention statement for my home. In the blink of an eye, my intention to live in the ocean breeze and to transition into work I loved became a reality.

There is so much power in creating a clear vision and documenting your specific intentions for your life. I've seen the magic manifest over and over again with my clients. Once they have channeled their hopes, desires, and dreams into a life plan that contains clearly and passionately articulated intentions, choices and actions, things start to happen.

I look forward to our first follow-up coaching calls, usually a week or so after we've completed the creation of their life plan. Inevitably, my clients are gushing in awe and wonder at the amazing series of events that have occurred, the renewed energy and joy they have for life, and the depth of their inner peace. They are feeling a wonderful sense of empowerment and mastery over their lives. I have to tell you there is no greater high for me than to know I am living my vision and purpose and making a profound difference in the lives of my clients!

Create Your Own Inspired Life Design

When an architect designs a home, it starts with a vision but is followed up with a highly detailed blueprint for each element that goes into the construction of the house. Think of yourself as the architect of your life. You can approach the design of your life in a haphazard way and just accept what shows up, or you can create a life that is purposeful and inspired. Having experienced both approaches in my own life, I have become quite the advocate for taking the time to create an inspired life design—a life plan that sings with energy, positive feeling and rock-solid intention.

An inspired life design flows naturally from your personal vision. When you are clear, connected, and excited about who you are, and what will bring meaning to your life, it's easy to take the next steps to create your life plan. It becomes a matter of consciously choosing the elements to support your vision in building a life that really works for you. The life plan you create becomes your blueprint to carry out the design of your life. What elements will serve as the building blocks of your life design? Here are some categories to think about when choosing the elements to include in your life plan:

Career/Business	Life Partner
Family	Travel/Vacations
Helpful People	Home
Friends	Creativity
Health	Lifework
Passionate Pursuits	Marriage
Pets	Creative Expression/Hobbies
Spirituality	Extended Family
Body	Personal Growth/Learning
Fame/Recognition	Self/Self-care/Self-acceptance
Children/Family	Service/Contribution
Play/Fun/Relaxation	Prosperity/Wealth
Wisdom/Knowledge	Emotional Well-being
Intellectual Stimulation	

Think of your life as a pie containing eight segments. Draw the pie of your life on a piece of paper. Looking at the above list, pick a label that best describes the eight most important aspects of your life. What aspects of your life need an infusion of energy in order to bring you to a quality of life that inspires you? Label each segment with words that have meaning for you, borrowing from the list above, or creating your own. You'll want this pie to be a picture of the fully robust and vibrant life you'd like to create for yourself. An effective and inspiring life plan will offer a nice balance between your work pursuits and those things that will significantly enhance the way you feel about your life.

As you finish labeling the pie of your life, ask yourself, "If all these aspects of my life are working, will I have a satisfying life?" If not, keep revising the picture of your pie until it feels complete. Everyone's pie chart will be different depending on the things you wish to emphasize in your life. Certainly you can find many more than eight aspects of your life that are important; however, at this point, it is helpful to focus on doing a few things well rather than overwhelming yourself with too many areas to think about.

Once you have identified the building blocks of your life plan, you will start the process of creating a powerful intention statement for each one. An intention statement is really very straightforward. It's not too different from creating a standard goal or objective statement with one very important exception. By going through the Stepping Stone process, you have gained the clarity about what is truly important to you. You are creating a plan that comes from the heart and NOT from a place of "I should." This is a huge, huge difference. Failure to follow up on goals and objectives, or New Year's resolutions, is common because most of the time they come from the head rather than the heart. They often come from the ugly inner critic holding a whip over you rather than the loving inner coach cheering you on to get something you really want, for the right reasons.

Most people don't spend a great deal of time finessing the words they use in a typical statement of goals and objectives and, as a result, the effort just doesn't do the job of energizing you to follow through and take action. A life plan constructed as an outcome of the awareness you have gained throughout the Stepping Stone process, that uses just the right words, is going to be supercharged with positive energy, and practically take on a life of its own.

Intention statements are like mini vision statements focused on a specific aspect of your life. Like your personal vision statement, an intention statement can start with the words "I am ____," or, if you prefer, you can start them by saying, "My intention is to____."

Start by picking one of your elements, such as your Creativity. Ask yourself, "What do I want to do, be or have? How do I want to go about achieving it?" "How will I feel when I have achieved it?" When I'm working with clients, we use a large whiteboard and just brainstorm words and phrases that capture the essence of what is desired. Then we will craft a statement that addresses all three of the above questions in words that are clear, powerful, and energizing for the client. It is important to state the intention in positive terms and in the present. You want to "act as if." Again, you want to phrase your intentions as a reflection of *what you want*, not *what you don't want*.

Examples of Powerful Intention Statements

In order to stimulate your thinking about how you might construct your own intention statements, I am including a collection of various intention statements created by my clients. Notice the variety, the energy, and the power in these statements.

Here are some examples of intention statements for **Creativity:**

> My intention is to create a space for mentally stimulating and artistically gratifying activities that satisfy my heart's desires and fire up my soul.

> I am giddy with childlike wonder, exploring multiple facets, kindred spirits and playful possibilities. It's like Christmas every day!
>
> I am birthing my book with love, joy, and magnificent creative energy that flows effortlessly through me.

All three statements are written to emphasize how it feels when the intention becomes reality. The statement itself uplifts and creates a new and powerfully delicious expectation for an area of life that had up to this point been lacking for the client. The first intention statement for creativity led my client to the creation of a product that she has since built into a very successful business, one that is profitable, fun, and deeply satisfying for her.

Here are some examples of intention statements for attracting a **Life Partner:**

> I am sharing an intimate soul connection; a fluid and mutually enriching journey that is playful, passionate, and stimulating.
>
> My intention is to enjoy a tender, loving, romantic, playful, uplifting, mutually fulfilling, and supportive relationship that continually grows and improves.
>
> I am building a loving & joyful relationship with myself. From a position of strength, wholeness, and empowerment, I am attracting and choosing a life partner who complements and enriches my life. We cherish each other.

That last one netted my client an exciting new man in her life in less than a week after her retreat experience with me in Santa

Barbara! She had arrived with the belief that she was unattractive to men and left radiating a glow that prompted a man she met in her travels to exclaim, "You are so beautiful! Will you have dinner with me?" Cautiously, she accepted, and embarked on the adventures of dating again.

Here are some examples of intention statements for **Fun or Play:**

> My intention is to, with a magical childlike sense of wonder, allow myself to have fun wherever I am and with whatever I want to do.

> I am energized and balanced, experiencing fun and laughter; joyfully achieving new heights of pleasure through new activities, people, and places. The world is my playground.

> My intention is to celebrate myself! To dance with pleasure and delight as I fulfill my need for adventure and exploration, stimulation, and exhilaration...and FUN!

All three of these intention statements were created by women who had been in a place of extreme burnout in their job, their life, or both. All three had been consumed by either pervasive negativity or sadness prior to beginning our work together. Can't you just feel the exuberant energy and excitement these women now have for their lives? One of them called me, a week after creating her life plan, to say, "Lauren, pardon my French, but I'm so (expletive deleted) HAPPY!" The surge of energy she experienced while creating her intentions for her life carried over into real life and she was ecstatic about her new experience of life as a joyful and fun place to be.

One of these clients disappeared for a month and I was concerned because I hadn't heard from her. When she reappeared, she informed me she'd very spontaneously taken advantage of a low airfare and the keys to a friend's car and condo in Sydney and spent a month traveling throughout Australia! Another of these clients took a two-week vacation on the Big Island in Hawaii, again finding rent-free accommodations. Amazing transformations happen when you give yourself permission to play and really enjoy life! Both returned high on life, with a renewed energy for carrying out the details of their life plans.

Here are some examples of intention statements for **Body/Health/Self-care:**

> I am vibrantly healthy, nurturing my mind, body, and spirit daily and experiencing balance, love, peace, and joy.

> I am honoring my body and mind through self-nurturing and a balanced lifestyle of physical fitness, healthy diet, and meditation.

> My intention is to create and maintain robust and vibrant physical health as an expression of the purposeful integration of my heart, mind, body, and spirit.

Too often we come to accept lethargy, fatigue, and being overweight and out of shape as just the way it is. At least all the evidence in our lives may have been pointing to a rather bleak reality. The power in creating an intention statement like any one of the above is that it will shift your expectation and you will begin to see possibility through eyes that have become empowered with a strong sense of mastery over your own destiny.

When you are firmly grounded in a positive, exciting intention you will find making the choices and taking the actions necessary to carry out your intention happen very easily. You will truly shift into an empowered place. I have had clients lose twenty pounds or more, with ease they never imagined possible. I've had clients say that long-term chronic pain that no doctor could ever explain, just went away. I've had clients who had dreaded exercise because they "hate going to the gym" create a fun and satisfying fitness program that they find easy to maintain. With intention, you can tackle even the gnarliest issue in your life and look forward to achieving success!

Here are some examples of intention statements for **Self-acceptance:**

> I am awakening to joy and passion with a sense of discovery through self-acceptance and self-nurturing.
>
> I am confident and unstoppable, thriving on self-love and appreciation; nurturing myself through gentle, loving and supportive thoughts, beliefs and actions.
>
> I am nurturing self-love and acceptance, feeling light and buoyant, jumping with joy and basking in serenity.

In my opinion, this is the gold right here. Finding that place of self-acceptance and the commitment to appreciate your gifts, your strengths, and your wonderful qualities and to accept with gentle compassion all of your humanness and imperfections—this will propel you further than you can imagine toward achieving your dreams. It really does start with you and giving yourself credit for all the richness and capabilities that you possess.

The area of self-acceptance is often the most difficult for many of my clients to embrace; however, it is also the one with the greatest impact in transforming your life. It's the self-hate, the self-flagellation, the contemptuous way we talk to ourselves that holds us in a place of misery, keeping us stuck in a status quo that only delivers more pain. I encourage everyone to put some real energy into building an intention for self-acceptance as an indispensable foundational building block upon which everything else will grow and blossom.

Here are some examples of intention statements for **Home:**

> My intention is to provide a beautiful and nurturing environment filled with harmony, for myself and others—an environment that feeds my soul.

> I am secure, nurtured and inspired; enveloped in comfort, tranquility, and sensual elegance.

> My intention is to live in a beautiful, peaceful, comfortable, and nurturing environment—a haven for myself, family and friends—balancing fun and entertainment with personal space and quiet time.

Home is where the heart is. Taking time to create a space that nurtures you, is pleasing, and provides comfort and tranquility is a great gift to give yourself and a wonderful investment in supporting your well-being and gaining the kind of quality of life that feels good to you.

Creating intention statements like the ones above, will bring your attention and focus to an area that may have been easy to neglect. Putting time, money, and energy into developing a nurturing personal space may have fallen victim to the belief that it was a frivolous use of resources (coming from that old belief that I'm not worth it!) Having intentions like these truly influences your choices and actions. If it's important to you, make it an intention. Things happen amazingly fast and easily when you put your mind to it.

Here are some examples of intention statements for **Career:**

> I am content and soulfully satisfied, making a bountiful contribution in my field, and waking up with awe, wonder, and exuberant passion every day.

> I am a career dynamo—an army of one— confidently achieving ever-greater success and satisfaction.

> My intention is to create my own company—an enterprise that is health-oriented, soul satisfying, and planet uplifting.

Whether you desire to improve your standing in your current career, change to a radically new career, or become your own boss by starting your own business, stating your intention clearly with powerful feeling words will propel you efficiently in the right direction. A clear statement of intention is the first step toward making it happen.

You don't need to know the specifics of the career you want at this stage, you only need to be clear about the quality of experience you desire to achieve and then make choices in support of gathering more information, experience, and knowledge that will bring even more clarity as detailed ideas and opportunities begin to emerge. With intention, you will find that in time, the career that makes your heart sing will reveal itself with glorious fanfare. And more often than not, you'll find that everything you've ever done in your life has prepared you for this moment. And when the time is right, and you are clear and motivated, everything falls into place with ease. One of my clients said it best after completing her life plan and gaining clarity about her career direction:

> "What appeared to have been unfortunate events in my life transformed themselves through this process into purposeful situations that I could not have planned nor imagined in my wildest dreams! Every single person, place and thing fits sensibly and magically together—forming the new, beautiful and bountiful fabric of my life! Just like Dorothy in the Wizard of Oz, I have an amazing journey that awaits—and a yellow brick road to follow!"

Choices and Actions

Hopefully you now have enough examples to get the idea how to go about creating your own set of powerful intention statements. Please remember that you are uniquely you and your intention statements will reflect that uniqueness. Take some time with this process. Don't think you should be able to whip all eight of them out in an hour! When I work with clients, we'll spend an hour or more working to create each individual intention statement. We take that kind of time to brainstorm what she really wants and to get the words just right. We want each statement to elicit a feeling of strong positive energy, because that's the kind of statement that is going to continue to energize you next week, next month, and even next year. So don't rush through this process. Set aside time to really think about it, to play with words and really bring your focused attention to the creation of your intentions. Whether you can spend an hour a day, an hour a week, or set aside a whole day for the process, please stick with it until you have created an energizing intention statement for every element that you listed on your pie of life.

For each intention statement, you will also create a series of choices and list your commitments to action. This is the part where the rubber meets the road, where you capture the details that will guide your actions over the next several months to a year. Your choices and actions will be the part you will update on a regular basis; as you complete one set of activities, you'll move on to the next level. As some of your choices become solidly entrenched new habits, you'll want to put emphasis on new and more challenging choices to bring you an even greater quality of life.

Look at each one of your intention statements and ask yourself, "Now that I am clear about my intention for my body, what choices will I make in daily life to ensure that I am on track with this intention?" Using the word "choice" goes back to our discussion about empowering language. We are talking about creating your personal life plan, for living an inspired life of your own design. That means you and only you are in charge of the choices you make. Forget about the "shoulds." If something makes your list because somebody else thinks you should, or you think someone else expects it of you, or because your inner critic is holding court in your head…stop and think again. In reality, an item like this will go the way of New Year's resolutions. You'll make a show of an effort, but if it isn't coming from your heart and from a place of your own choosing, there is no point in wasting space writing it down! It will just clutter up your plan and be a drag on your energy. Only put things in your plan that you truly, deeply desire to do for your own well-being. You'll be motivated, energized and amazingly productive in carrying out a plan that comes from the heart.

Each choice you make will then be further supported by a list of specific and measurable actions. Many of these actions may have made your to-do lists in the past, but this time, they are in the context of your personal vision and your intention for a particular aspect of your life. They are supporting items for you to carry out specific choices you have made that come directly from your heart! That's a big difference from having a laundry list of things to do that don't reflect your priorities or your personal choices.

Having a comprehensive life plan created in this way, naturally clarifies your priorities. It will become easier to evaluate whether an action or a request coming from an outside source will be something you say "Yes" to or not. It will become so much easier to say "No" to the things that do not fit into the design of your life!

Here's how it looks when you put it all together:

My Intention:

> I am honoring my body and mind through self-nurturing and a balanced lifestyle of physical fitness, healthy diet, and relaxation.

My Choices:

> Take time to meditate each day
>
> Eat more fruits and vegetables
>
> Exercise in ways that are fun for me

My Commitment to Action:

> Listen to a meditation CD each night before bed
>
> Shop at the Farmer's Market on Wednesdays at lunchtime

Pack a healthy lunch to take to work
each day

Rollerblade at the park two days a
week after work

Join a Pilates class that meets twice a week

When your life plan is complete, you will have your personal vision and purpose statement first, followed by eight sections that look like the above, one for each element of the pie chart you made earlier. You can see that your life plan doesn't have to be a very lengthy document. It may be deceptively short when all is said and done, considering the amount of time and energy put into it. However, every word will have meaning and the energy that you'll feel every time you read it will motivate you to stay focused and in action, moving forward with joyful anticipation as you create the life you have envisioned for yourself.

Think of your life plan as a living, breathing document. It is not intended to be something set in concrete, and therefore rigid and inflexible. As you start to take actions, new opportunities will present themselves; opportunities for new choices and actions and for tweaking your game plan. As you complete your action steps, you'll want to continuously add the next level of detail to your plan.

Your vision and your intentions are created at a level that may last you for years. Your choices and actions will need to be revisited on a regular basis. Revisit your intentions once a year to see if you want to add new intentions for other areas that are emerging in importance to you. Perhaps you feel you've sufficiently achieved an intention to the point you no longer need to put energy into making it happen because it has become something you no longer need to think about. Revisit your choices and actions on a monthly, if not weekly, basis.

Armed with your new life plan, it becomes very easy to make choices and decisions when faced with a dilemma. It's a matter of asking yourself a few simple questions. Does this decision fit with the vision and intentions I hold for my life? If I make this choice, will it further my progress toward the future I envision? It becomes incredibly easy to determine what to do and what not to do, and to evaluate next steps on your journey.

Now if you write out your life plan and toss it in a drawer, never to be heard from or seen again, it's not going to be as effective as it could be. I believe just the act of creating your intentions alone and committing them to paper will create some amazing results for you. But in time, if you do not keep your intentions front and center, reading them on a regular basis and tweaking your plan as you go, it will cease to bring its magic to your life. Your life plan will transform your life, but only if you continue to put your energy into reviewing it and working it. As it is said in business, plan your work and work your plan. In this case, design your life and go out and live it!

In Stepping Stone Seven, our final guidepost on the journey, we will look at ways to stay true to your vision and to stay focused on implementing your new life plan, even if you experience some bumps in the road.

◆ Stepping Stone Seven:

Staying True to Your Vision
Navigating the bumps in the road

> *"This above all: To thine own self be true."*
>
> –William Shakespeare

Now that you have an inspiring life plan, you'll feel invincible, excited, exuberant, and full of hope and possibility for a future of your own design. This energy will propel you forward indefinitely, as long as you maintain a clear focus. Staying true to your vision and purpose, your intentions, and the choices and actions you have committed to, will bring your dreams into reality.

All too often, inspiration is fleeting. We'll get inspired by something we watch on TV, a book we've read, or a workshop we've attended, and we'll get energized for a week or two, then our enthusiasm wanes and we are right back to the status quo. In this chapter we'll talk about some simple tools and support strategies you can use to maintain your focus and stay the course for the long haul.

Implementing Your Life Plan

When you are feeling energized and inspired by your new life plan, you will probably feel highly motivated to start making things happen. You've got the vision; you've got the clarity of your intentions and a clear set of choices and a whole lot of action waiting to be taken. And things will start happening quickly. There is an element of adrenaline going on and once you've used up that natural high, you may find your pace slowing down. You may become frustrated at not being able to change everything all at once or disappointed that you can't maintain such an elevated momentum. It's easy to expect too much of yourself right away. It's a common scenario and time for a reminder to be gentle with yourself. Rome was not built in a day! True and lasting transformation takes time.

A lot of what you've written in your plan will require you to establish some new habits. My recommendation is to tackle one new habit at a time. If you want to start a new exercise program…change your eating habits…have friends over once a week…go for hikes on the weekends…cook fresh foods…write each day in your journal…set aside a regular time for a hobby…and you want to do it perfectly starting right now—you are likely to end up overwhelmed and could relapse into beating yourself up for not following through. Take it easy. Pick the most important new habit and integrate it into your life. Experience some success with one new habit, and then add another. Experience success with two new habits, and then add another. Keep on integrating new habits into your life one by one and it won't be long at all before you will be living a life that really works for you and you will be very proud of yourself indeed.

You may have created one or more intentions for your life that may take years to achieve. It can be harder to stay focused and easier to become overwhelmed when the goal is a big one. This is particularly true if you have to keep one foot in the old reality while you are trying to create the new. For example, if you have created an intention to make a major change in your life—like starting a new business—and you've got a full-time job, kids to take care of, a household to manage, and a significant other to nurture too, you can pretty easily start to second-guess yourself and feel overwhelmed by the magnitude of the challenge that lies before you. It's important to remember to pace yourself, and to choose small deliberate steps, one at a time in a way that will fit into your life without turning it upside down.

I have a story I love to tell about my own experience of being easily overwhelmed. When I was a child, my father was in business for himself as an insurance agent. I remember being five or six years old and so proud that my daddy would let me help him in his office. He would often give me a small stack of index cards to alphabetize. I felt so important! Well, one day, as he was about to give me another little stack of cards, the phone rang, so he absent-mindedly handed me the whole pile and left the room to take the call. When he returned, he found me crying. "What's the matter, honey?" he asked gently. I looked at him with big innocent eyes and wailed, "IT'S TOO BIG!" He looked at me in confusion, and then realized I had been overwhelmed by the size of the stack of cards he had handed me. "Oh, I see," he said. He took back the huge pile of cards and peeled off a tiny little section of cards and gave them back to me. I smiled a big smile and went back to happily alphabetizing the cards.

As I got older and school projects threatened to paralyze me, my dad would always remind me of this little story. I can't tell you how many times in my life I have called on this memory to help me get through an overwhelming project. In fact even now as I set about the task of writing this book I've remembered that advice. Thinking of putting 50,000 words to paper kept this book on the back burner for over a year, but thinking of it as a series of 1,000 word stories got my project off and running and feeling like so much fun! No matter how big and daunting a goal you set for yourself, it can always be broken down into smaller bite-size pieces.

There is a movie called *What About Bob?* in which Bill Murray plays a man who is nearly paralyzed by his fears. His psychiatrist gives him a book called *Baby Steps* and encourages him to focus on very small steps that are non-threatening. It's a wonderful metaphor for achieving big goals in life. If the goal is aggressive, the magnitude of the actions required to achieve it can seem overwhelming and you can slip into paralysis. It is so important to give yourself permission to go at your own pace and to value the baby steps. Over time a series of baby steps add up to an enormous leap forward. The woman who commits to tiny increments of forward movement over a long period of time will get where she wants to go in time. Time is always on your side.

Keeping Yourself on Track

As you get started with your new life plan, it is important to have a strategy for keeping on track. Oftentimes in business, the boss requires a weekly status report to track progress toward goals, to give a heads-up when things are getting off course, and to indicate what activities you plan for the coming week. You are the boss of your life, so it's a good idea to give yourself status reports on your life goals. To formalize the process, so it doesn't fall by the wayside when other demands jockey for attention, schedule a "staff meeting" with yourself once a week at the same time, on the same day each week. Make this your sacred time for reaffirming your vision, reviewing your life plan, assessing your progress, and planning your next steps. I like to keep the format simple:

Review of Last Week:

Wins/Accomplishments/Insights:

Challenges and Obstacles:

What needs attention?

Plan for Next Week:

What do I want to accomplish?

What are my top three priorities for the week?

What will I do to take care of myself?

If you are going to be the boss of your life, how about being a benevolent boss? No abuse allowed! The point of having a progress report is not to beat yourself up for anything you haven't done. It's to keep you aware of what needs more attention and to notice and acknowledge the progress that you are making. To keep your momentum going, it's important to celebrate your wins!

It is essential to keep your commitments to yourself if you want to succeed in creating what you want in life. It is, however, equally important to be reasonable in the expectations you set for yourself. Experiencing small successes will propel you further over the long run than burning yourself out quickly by trying to do too much too fast. Remember the overall objective is to create a pleasing quality of life!

I observe it over and over again with my clients: the tendency to be hard on herself for failing to achieve something she set out to do, when she said she was going to do it...forgetting to notice the long list of things she did accomplish! As women we tend to be guilty of setting our expectations for ourselves very high and then focusing on the one thing we didn't get around to doing rather than celebrating the twenty things we checked off our list.

As you embark on this amazing journey of transformation, give yourself the gift of acknowledgement. Notice the progress you make each day, each week, each month, each year. Make a point of celebrating even the smallest baby steps. Baby steps move you forward and it doesn't take but a few baby steps to add up to a significant stride.

It is important to create a habit of documenting your accomplishments. When you are feeling discouraged, a quick read of your accomplishments will remind you that you are in fact moving steadily toward your goal. Keep your progress reports in a file or a binder for easy access, to review and remind yourself how far you have come!

Everybody is going to have ups and downs. Some days you'll be like a whirling dervish getting things done with speed and efficiency. Other days you might feel uninspired or just tired and unable to focus. Instead of beating yourself up for it, remind yourself that tomorrow is another day and that, for whatever reason, today you just needed to take it easy.

For clients that struggle with maintaining focus, you might need a bit more handholding from the "boss." I recommend daily check-ins with yourself to supplement your weekly planning and review sessions. Depending on what works best for the individual, this can be done at the end of the day, reviewing today and planning tomorrow; or, you can do it at the beginning of each day, reviewing yesterday and planning today. Again, the format is simple:

Regarding Yesterday (or Today)
What worked?

What didn't work?

Insights:

Preparing for Today (or Tomorrow)
What three things do I want to accomplish?

What actions will ensure balance?

Other To Do items to capture for later:

These tools are meant to support you, so feel free to adapt them to your particular needs. But do keep it simple and do use them. Maintaining energy for the long-haul depends on being able to see where you've been, being clear on next steps, and knowing you are that much closer to your goal!

The Challenge with Change

When you grow and blossom into the person you've always dreamed of being, sometimes the people around you can't keep up. They want to, perhaps, but what drives you internally can be baffling to others. When you establish a relationship, whether a friendship, a family tie, or a love relationship, you create a dynamic based on who you are in the moment, and some people don't want to see anything change.

As you charge forward in making your dreams come alive, be aware that important people in your life may become uncomfortable, even jealous of what you are doing. Or, what you are doing may just scare them to death. They may fear you will no longer need them or love them if you take this new direction in life. It takes great courage to make changes that rock the boat. Most people do not have that kind of courage and will offer up all kinds of reasons why what you are doing will not work.

The irony is that now that you've muzzled your inner naysayer, the outer naysayers seem to pick up steam! And heaven forbid, you are feeling fear, uncertainty and doubt, or you've experienced a failure or disappointment in getting the results you expected. You'll find no shortage of people to be right there, saying, "Yeah, maybe it's time to face reality and let go of this pipe dream of yours." Just remember to let your inner knowing be your guide and trust the intuition that has brought you this far.

As you grow and change, your needs change. Some people in your life may not be able to adjust to the new you, and as such, tension and turmoil begin to emerge. Certain people may no longer fit. In fact, the person who seemed to be the wind beneath your wings can suddenly seem to be throwing sand on your wings and holding you back. The shift can be subtle and build over time. At some level you may be aware of the change, but more likely there will be a sudden wake-up call. It may be necessary to revisit the relationship, set boundaries, or even let the relationship go.

There is always something to learn in difficult situations. Look to see if the way this person is treating you may in fact be the way you are treating yourself unconsciously. This can be a message that you need to do more work on your inner belief system. Or it can be that this person simply does not see and appreciate the person you have become.

The truth is what sets you free. There is no substitute for honest, direct communication. In the end, what is right for you is going to be what is right for others around you. If you do not communicate clearly what you need and what you require for your relationship to work, you are not allowing the important people in your life the opportunity to choose to step up to the plate and give it to you! And if their choice is to ignore your needs or throw roadblocks in your path, then step up to the plate yourself and make some decisions. Ask yourself whether you are better off with or without this person in your life. Can you pull away from the relationship enough to give yourself the space to do what you need to do, or will you have to take the step to move on and leave this person behind?

Sometimes the only change required is for you to stop taking things personally. Learn to observe the difficult behavior of others from a more detached place. Learn to recognize when it's their stuff and choose not to engage. Learn to allow them to be who they are, as you would like them to allow you to be who you are. Let go of the need to convince anyone that you know what you are doing. Say, "I'll think about what you've said," "I appreciate your concern," or "I'll take that into consideration." You don't need their permission to do what you have determined is right for you. You can agree to disagree. If someone is giving you a hard time, realize it's their stuff and you don't have to take it on. There is a lot of peace in letting go of the need to control what other people think or how they behave.

Disappointments and Detours

When we are working toward fulfilling our dreams, oftentimes "real life" does intervene, and circumstances can send you into a temporary tailspin. Temporary is the operative word here. Life happens. It just does. Events and circumstances don't always line up the way we would consciously choose. Resilience, perseverance and commitment will bring you back on track.

The secret to staying focused is to wear your vision like a bullet-proof vest. Yes, it hurts to get shot, and even if you're wearing the vest, taking a bullet will knock you out cold, but you'll regain consciousness soon enough and find your body bruised, but still intact. And you'll be so grateful to be alive!

By now, you may be thinking that everything I've wanted or asked for since I embarked on my journey to give wings to my dreams, has come to pass easily and effortlessly. Perhaps I've got that Midas touch and everything I set out to accomplish turns to gold. Well, not exactly.

I have not been a perfect implementer of my own advice and newfound wisdom, nor have I been immune to unexpected and undesirable circumstances. There have been some unpleasant bumps in the road. I've taken a few detours and had a few setbacks. The strength of my vision has helped me stay the course. As any sailor knows, the best way to get where you are going is rarely a straight line. You've just got to keep your eye on the destination and know that with perseverance you will eventually get where you want to go.

A little over a year after moving to Santa Barbara, my relationship with the man in my life came to an end, and it rocked my world. We had been together for six years but had been drifting apart. We had what seemed like an otherworldly connection—when words were not required our communication was awesome. We seemed to share a sort of ESP kind of knowing. But when it came to ordinary human communication, we were the proverbial

Venus and Mars. We had a deeply loving relationship—but one in which we could never fully commit to each other.

He had been there for me, comforting me through the trauma and drama of my ex-husband's drug addiction. He had cheerfully stayed with my kids while I went off to workshops, retreats, and coach training classes. My boys adored him and he loved my boys. Though neither of us really wanted to end it, we hit a wall and there seemed to be no other choice. The decision was painful, and even though it was mutual, it broke my heart.

When the relationship ended, I was temporarily derailed. There was no way I could move forward until I processed my pain. While I was grieving, the gremlins of fear, uncertainty, and doubt were doing a number on me. I began to question my choices and my direction. During this time, I relied heavily on writing in my journal, the support of my family and friends, and the invaluable assistance of another coach to get me through the pain. In time, I worked through the grief, and I was able to see my life from a new perspective. My vision gathered even more strength and my determination to move forward resumed with gusto, and I began to channel my energy into the joyful process of writing this book.

You can experience great success implementing new habits and taking concrete steps in a new direction, having a plan and working the plan—and then suddenly something comes out of left field to completely knock you off course. It may temporarily cloud your vision. It's a scary place when you can't see past the end of your nose. When things happen that aren't part of the plan, that we wouldn't have chosen, it's important to know that it's just a bump in the road—even if that bump seems more like a deep and alarming pothole.

Perhaps you've heard of the legendary road to Negril. Negril is the home of a number of fabulous tropical beach resorts in Jamaica. The road is paved now, but it used to be a dizzying journey to get to your resort once you arrived on the island. The road trip was full of unsettling twists and turns, bumps and bruises, and you'd wonder if you'd get there in one piece. Once you arrived, you'd have no doubt the journey was worth it, but you would experience some fear, uncertainty, and doubt along the way.

Following your dreams is very much like that. No matter how passionate we are about our direction, how diligent we've been in handling our inner critic, how clear we are about what we want to achieve, there will no doubt be bumps in the road that will challenge our resolve.

There is a child's rhyme about going on a bear hunt and coming up to a series of obstacles—a deep cold river, a big dark forest, a scary dark cave—if you can't go over it, and you can't go under it, you've got to go through it! The key is to find a way to keep moving forward.

Sometimes the bumps in the road are generated internally—as in getting swallowed up by fear or losing your confidence. Sometimes the bumps are generated externally, such as when unexpected events or difficult people create roadblocks. And then there are the times when life just throws you curve balls. You are moving joyfully forward when something comes out of nowhere and you've got no choice but to stop and deal with it.

When faced with an event or circumstance that seems to derail you, remember that nothing has changed about your vision, your values, or your passions. You've only lost your focus temporarily. Take the time to deal with the turmoil, process your emotions, and get yourself centered again. This is a good time to revisit Stepping Stone One to refuel your tank and renew your spirit.

When you've got your mojo back, know you can get right back on the horse and pick up where you left off. Dreams are resilient— they will wait for you!

Reaching Out for Support

You might notice a theme throughout my personal journey and that is that I have always reached out for help. Whether through reading books, attending workshops and retreats, hiring coaches, or joining support groups, I've always been a seeker. Seeking to find the right help at the right time. I'm not a workshop groupie, but I do challenge myself to grow and learn and to reach for support from outside myself when I feel stuck. When I have allowed myself to reach out for support, I have always found it right around the corner as if it were just sitting there waiting for me to ask.

I have shared with you a number of pivotal experiences in my life journey, in hopes that it will inspire you to reach out for help and support as well. It's not necessary, nor very effective, to try to do everything alone or to figure out all the answers by yourself. I hope this book has been a very good start for you, and please know there is more help available. Trust your instincts and notice when an awareness of a resource or an opportunity crosses your path. It might be just what you need to move you forward.

In coaching school, rule number one is "Every coach has a coach." That may surprise you, but even highly trained and experienced coaches hire coaches for themselves because there is great value in having someone outside yourself to ask you questions, listen deeply and offer observations, ideas, and support. Coaches are human too and we need support just like anyone else. It's not so easy to be the unbiased listener and observer when it's your own life you are looking at! Hiring a coach is an investment you make in yourself, that will support you in achieving the dreams you hold dear.

A life coach can help you work through the Stepping Stones outlined in this book, to help you reach the clarity of having your vision and purpose and a life plan. Once you've discovered your vision and have created your life plan, a coach can be a valuable partner, helping you to stay on track. Staying true to your vision requires focus, time, and effort, all of which can easily fall by the wayside when demands of daily life intervene. Setting aside a regular time to talk with your coach will ensure that you keep moving forward and you'll have a dedicated, unbiased partner to support you in your journey.

If hiring a coach isn't an option for you, consider starting a support group. You probably know, or could easily find, other women in the same boat who could use a little sisterhood. You can form a study group using this book and support each other through the Stepping Stone process. A few simple rules are important to follow. Listen without judgment. Offer suggestions without any attachment as to whether they are accepted and followed. Each member is best served by focusing her energy on her own journey. Getting too wrapped up in another's journey is a way to avoid focusing on your own! Gently remind each other to use empowering, positive language and to leave negativity at the door. Create some rules of engagement together as a group and commit to respecting those rules. Take turns bringing refreshments and have fun!

Revisit the Stepping Stones

Each time we embark on a quest for personal growth, we learn something new, we make new discoveries about ourselves, we adopt new beliefs and we engage in new behaviors. It's an incremental process and life continues to be an adventure of new learning. The Stepping Stone process is intended to be something you can revisit again and again, each time taking your learning to a new level.

If you find yourself tired, or facing a new kind of turmoil, revisit Stepping Stone One, *Refueling Your Tank and Renewing Your Spirit,* and recommit to your self-care and nurturing. If you find yourself feeling stuck and having trouble moving forward, revisit Stepping Stone Three, *Believing You Can Have What You Want,* and take a look to see if your inner critic might be engaging in self-sabotage tactics. If you find you have slipped away from joyful anticipation and into frustration, negative expectation, and seeing the glass half empty, revisit Stepping Stone Four, *Feeling Your Way to a Better Life,* and work to reconnect with ways to find joy in the journey. If you find yourself moving at top speed and implementing your life plan with ease, hurray for you! You may want to revisit Stepping Stone Six, *Harnessing the Power of Intention,* on a frequent basis to challenge yourself to create new and even more exciting intentions for yourself. The Stepping Stone process works. It worked for me and it has worked for my clients. And it will work for you! Revisit them as needed to keep your momentum going.

Patience, Patience, Patience

Napoleon Hill tells a story in the book *Think and Grow Rich* about an ambitious gold miner who toiled for many months looking for a vein of gold. Frustrated and weary, he gave up. Soon after, another miner discovered the gold vein just three feet away from where the first miner decided to throw in the towel! This is such a great reminder that sometimes impatience gets in the way of perseverance! There are likely to be moments of doubt and times when you feel discouraged. When this happens, just imagine the vein of gold being just around the corner and strengthen your resolve to hang in there!

There will be moments of magic and likely some moments of frustration along the journey. You might move at rocket speed or you may meander. Most people who appear to be overnight successes, probably invested many years of focused effort, trial and error, and perseverance and commitment, behind the scenes, before they achieved the success that everyone thinks happened overnight. Putting in the daily effort, keeping your focus on what you can do today to bring you closer to where you want to be, and keeping your eye on the big vision will reap rewards in time.

It's like climbing a mountain. You can't quite see your final destination until you get very near the top, but knowing it's there keeps you going. In order to make it to the peak, you've got to keep putting one foot in front of the other, paying careful attention to your footing at each step along the way. The small steps aren't necessarily glamorous, but you can't make it to the top without them! Celebrate your progress along the way, and know that the small steps will get you there in time!

Make a commitment to yourself to stay true to your vision—to navigate the bumps in the road and get back on track, to seek out support and use the tools to keep you focused and moving forward. Allow yourself to celebrate your wins, even the tiny little baby steps. Be patient and enjoy the unfolding of your new life.

You have reached the end of the Stepping Stone journey. Now it's time to spread your beautiful wings and fly!

◆ Epilogue:

The Wind Beneath Your Wings

Soaring with pure positive energy

"Go confidently in the direction of your dreams.
Live the life you have imagined."

–Henry David Thoreau

In December of 2003, I spent a week in Jamaica at a fun-loving and playful resort in Negril. The experience was pure magic. While I was there, I achieved an exciting personal milestone for myself. I learned to scuba dive! It was one of those highly charged "I can't" items from my list that I was determined to shift to an "I can."

I had a lot of fear associated with breathing underwater, probably due to the fact I had childhood asthma. In fact, I'd been told years before that I couldn't scuba dive because of my medical history. But I wanted so badly to experience the beauty and peacefulness of underwater landscapes and marine life. So I faced this fear head on, got medical clearance, signed up for classes at home, and headed to Jamaica to complete my certification dives.

I confess to moments of panic and came very close to refusing to go under during my first open water dive. But my instructor was gentle and persuasive and guided me firmly beneath the waves. Upon resurfacing, I felt both exuberance and nausea. I actually lost my breakfast in the choppy waves while waiting to be picked up by the dive boat. Embarrassing and unpleasant, but I persevered. I am now a certified PADI open water diver!

The highlight of my Jamaica diving experience was coming within a few feet of a Manta Ray with an eight-foot wingspan! I also got to swim with a sea turtle and multitudes of colorful fish. The variety of texture and color in the coral reef was exquisite. I was absolutely thrilled! This experience raised the bar for me. I now believe I can do just about anything I put my focus, intention, and commitment behind. And it always helps to have a gentle and persuasive professional at your side!

My trip to Jamaica was a turning point in my life for a much more important reason—it was a week in which I reconnected in a joyful and exuberant way with the man I truly and deeply love. Our relationship had been torn apart the year before, but the bond of our love remained rock solid. I had thought the magic was in Jamaica, but it turned out the magic was in our newfound, committed relationship. The magic came home with us.

On the first day of Spring in March 2004, we were married in the beautiful backyard garden of the home we now share in Santa Barbara. We stood between two trumpet trees that burst into full and vibrant golden bloom just for the occasion. We wrote our own vows, and tears of joy came to my eyes when we recited the words "I promise to love you just the way you are."

Our wedding day started out misty and overcast. I was caught up in our exchange of vows and didn't notice that something magical happened. My sister excitedly told me after the ceremony, that as the minister pronounced us husband and wife, the sun broke through the clouds, in a moment of spiritual splendor, bathing us in its ray of light! To top off a beautiful ceremony, each of our guests released a Monarch butterfly. We all watched in awe as they stretched their wings and took flight. The symbolism was extraordinary. We had given wings to our relationship dreams.

It is December 2005, just over eight years since that fateful day when I found myself a crumpled mess of fear and despair, caught in the middle of my ex-husband's methamphetamine drama. It seems like a lifetime ago and it seems like only yesterday. Eight years of baby steps and some huge leaps. Eight years of steady purposeful movement forward, sprinkled with a few bumps in the road and the occasional tailspin. But mostly, it's been eight years of awe and wonder, as I have experienced the unfolding of a triumphant journey.

As I write these final words of my book, I am overcome with emotion. I am living my dream and loving my life in ways I couldn't even imagine a few short years ago. Most exciting to me in this moment, is that my children are proud of me. They've been my inspiration and my source of strength and determination to stay true to my vision, and to stay the course I set forth in my life plan.

I have come to understand that true happiness comes from within. It comes from building a relationship with yourself that is grounded in love, respect and acceptance, a relationship you can count on no matter what your circumstances. It comes from honoring your needs, desires and dreams, and remembering to nurture the little girl within.

Happiness can seem elusive indeed when you are caught up in the throes of midlife turmoil. By following the Seven Stepping

Stone process and taking time to ponder the questions and pursue the suggested activities, I know you too will emerge triumphant!

When you shift your focus to hope and new beginnings, magical things start to happen. The journey starts with taking personal responsibility for the quality of your life, and making the choice to step into your power as a woman, willing to take charge and transform your life. You and only you are the architect of your life and the master of your destiny. I hope I have inspired you to grab the reins of your life and steer it in the direction of wherever it is that *you* want to go!

And always remember that the wind beneath your wings is in fact your own pure positive energy. If you want to soar higher, all you have to do is bring more positive feeling and focused energy to the forefront. It is there for you to harness and direct to do your bidding.

From the bottom of my heart I wish you a joyful journey and a pleasant flight as you give wings to your dreams!

Addendum:

Resources for Working the Stepping Stone Process

"Whatever you can do, or dream you can, begin it. Boldness has genius, power, and magic in it."

–Johann Wolfgang von Goethe

Questions to Ponder and Activities to Pursue

Perhaps you have read through this book with the intention of going back later to contemplate the questions in more depth and spend more time on the activities. The following pages offer you a convenient reference for you to revisit the Stepping Stones in your own time and at your own pace. All of the questions I have posed and the activities I have suggested throughout the book are summarized here.

Remember to enjoy the journey as you ponder these questions and pursue the activities that follow. Be patient with yourself and trust that the answers you are looking for will unfold beautifully as you embark on your quest to give wings to your dreams!

If you enjoy the structure of a workbook format, an even more comprehensive set of questions and activities, is available as a companion to this book. The *Give Wings To Your Dreams—Personal Journal and Activity Guide* can be purchased at www.GoldenWingsPress.com.

Part I: Honoring Your Needs, Desires and Dreams

Stepping Stone One:
Refueling Your Tank and Renewing Your Spirit
Shoring up your energy for change

- Start a personal journal. Write without judgment, anything that comes to mind: your thoughts and feelings, hopes and dreams, concerns and challenges, ideas and opportunities. What's working, what's not working in your life. Make a habit of writing daily entries in your journal, with a goal of writing three full pages each morning before you start your day or each evening before you go to bed. Use this journal to ponder the questions posed throughout the Stepping Stone process and to record insights and ideas.

- Engage in extreme self-care. Commit to doing the things that will rejuvenate your body and renew your spirit on a regular basis. Strive to do more than seems practical as you want to dramatically overcome the tendency toward self-neglect! Pay special attention to doing the things that would please you and give you a feeling of comfort and contentment, the intention being to create new habits for honoring your very real needs and nurturing yourself back to vibrant well-being. Practice saying "No" to create more personal time.
  - What do my body, mind, and spirit need right now to help me rejuvenate?
    - Find ways to play?
    - Spend time on a hobby?
    - Physical well-being?
    - Emotional well-being?

Mental stimulation?

Creative expression?

Spiritual connection?

Clear clutter?

Create personal space?

Enhance the aesthetics of my surroundings?

- Choose up to three areas listed above and make a list of things you will do for your own self-care over the next two weeks in these categories.

- Schedule "time off" just for you: What can I do to make time just for me on a regular basis? An hour a day? An hour twice a week? An afternoon a week? A getaway weekend? A week's vacation? Take a sabbatical?

Stepping Stone Two:
Getting In Touch With Your Deepest Desires
Resurrecting the dreams you left behind

- Go on a mental treasure hunt. Excavate clues that will help you reconnect with the things you love and identify your personal passions. Ask yourself the following questions and write the answers in your journal:
  - What do I really love?
  - What did I love at age five, age ten, age fifteen, age twenty?
  - What did I want to be when I grew up?
  - Who were my role models as a child? Who do I admire now?
  - What are the values I hold dear?
  - What are my top ten values? My top five values?

- Is the life I am living a reflection of my deepest values?

- What changes are important for me to bring my life more in balance with my values?

- What do I want more than anything in the world?

- If time, money, and resources were no object, what would I be doing with my life?

- What are twenty things that I want or desire?

- Do I believe I deserve what I want?

- Can I give myself permission to have what I want?

- Am I open to actually achieving or receiving all that I want?

- If you have difficulty with the above three questions, take your list of twenty things you want and for each item, write out the following three statements:

    I deserve (or I am worthy) to have_____.

    I give myself permission to have _____.

    I am open to having (or receiving) _____.

- Say the above statements out loud at least once a day until you feel very confident that you can indeed have what you want!

Part II: Creating an Inner Environment for Your Dreams to Flourish

Stepping Stone Three:

Believing You Can Have What You Want

Conquering your inner critic and limiting beliefs

- Find a quiet place where you can be alone with your journal for a little while. Ask yourself, "What are the ways I tell myself that I can't?" "What do I believe I can't be, do, or have?" Now ask yourself which of these beliefs are grounded in fact and which are fiction? Identify the statements that are not clearly a fact and rewrite them to read, "I can..." Better yet, "OH YES I CAN...!"

- What are the messages of your inner critic? Does it have a name? What does it look like? Speak in its language as you write about all of the harsh, pessimistic, and contemptuous messages that the stealth voice of your inner gremlin employs to keep you stuck in the status quo. What does it say when you say the words, "I am...?"

- Now examine each of these messages and decide if you want to own them or if you are ready to replace them with more deliberate, conscious, and positive messages that will serve to empower you to move forward in your life. Write out the messages you wish to have your new inner coach employ to keep you inspired and motivated to embrace the changes you seek for your life. Ask yourself, "How would I talk to a good friend or loved one who was beating herself up like this?" This is how you want your inner coach to talk to you! Give your inner coach a name that delights you and visualize a kind and supportive figure sitting on your shoulder, always there to cheer you on.

- Write down these positive messages as statements of affirmation and keep them in a place you will frequently notice them. Use note cards or sticky notes to post your empowering beliefs where you will see them. Pick one at a time and say it out loud to yourself throughout the day until you feel you have embraced it, then repeat the process with each new affirmation.

- Practice using empowering language and notice how it shifts your energy:

Replace	With
I should	I choose to, I desire to, I want to
I need to	It's important to me to
I have to	I desire to
I can't	I can or I'm not willing to
I'll try	I intend to
I always, I never	I sometimes, In the past, I

- Be compassionate with yourself. Let go of judgment about past choices. Practice forgiveness towards yourself and others.

- Avoid "black and white" thinking. Look for the shades of gray.

- What stops me from asking for help? In what ways would I like to get help? Who can I ask for help/support? How will I ask for it?

- What stops me from asking for what I need from my partner or other important person in my life? How would I benefit if this person understood my needs and gave me what I asked for? How would he/she benefit? What will I ask for?

- If these questions are very difficult for you and you feel stuck, consider working with a life coach to guide you through the process.

Stepping Stone Four:
Feeling Your Way To A Better Life
Finding joy in the journey

- Focus on what is working in your life rather than what is not working.

- Start a gratitude journal or incorporate expressions of gratitude in your daily journal writing practice

  - What am I grateful for?

  - What do I appreciate:
    About my partner?
    About my children?
    About my pet(s)?
    About extended family?
    About friends, acquaintances and associates?
    About my home?
    About the world around me?

  - What do I appreciate about me? Dedicate at least one entire page to this topic! When you are finished, read it out loud to yourself and bask in all that you appreciate about being you!

  - If there is a difficult person or situation in your life: write about aspects you can appreciate, the possible gifts in the situation, what you can learn from this, what you can do personally to improve the situation, even if the other party does nothing different. Notice if there is a shift in the energy in your interactions with this person or situation just by changing your focus!

◆ Remember a time you felt happy. Conjure up memories that bring you to a joyful place—perhaps something you experienced as a child or a young adult. Use your senses to imagine this happy time in as much detail as you can. Tap in to those positive feelings right now and let them lift your spirit. Go back to this memory any time you need a lift to bring yourself to a more positive feeling place.

◆Clear out negativity.

• Do a "burning bowl" exercise. On one or more pieces of paper (not your journal) write down all the negative feelings you would like to let go of to make room for more positive feelings. Be specific. Name each nuance of negative emotion you are feeling about anyone or anything in your life right now, including any negativity you direct at yourself. Begin your statements with the words: I release…, I forgive ___ for___, or I let go…

• When you feel complete with this exercise, toss it in your fireplace if you have one and watch it burn! If you don't have a safe place to actually burn it, tear your papers into little bits and toss them in the trash or insert them into a shredder.

◆ Once you have done your releasing ceremony to toss out the negativity in your life, consciously choose the positive feelings you want to fill your life with. Fill up at least one page in your journal with all the wonderful positive feelings you'd like to experience. Start your statements with, I choose to dwell in feelings of…, I choose to focus on…, I choose…, etc.

Part III: Bringing Your Dreams Into Reality

Stepping Stone Five:

Creating a Compelling Personal Vision
Imagining you are already where you want to be

- Spend some time daydreaming. Find a time and place where you won't be disturbed or distracted. Let your mind wander into a future that delights you. Use as many senses as you can to give your vision texture and richness. Notice how you feel when you imagine this new reality. Suspend judgment and don't worry about whether your ideas are practical; just allow yourself to dream. Keep your journal handy and record your ideas, images, and/or feelings in as much detail as possible.

- Create a picture collage that represents your dreams and desires for your life. Use a poster board or a scrapbook. Be creative and express yourself any way that pleases you in this project. Use words and pictures you cut from a magazine, greeting cards, or photographs, or draw your own pictures and illustrate with calligraphy. Let this be a joyful expression of who you are and where you are going. Remember to focus on what you want (without limitations) and be as specific as possible.

- Explore Feng Shui. If the idea of arranging items in your home as visual reminders of what you seek to create in your life appeals to you, then find a book on Feng Shui or hire a consultant to help you.

- Continue to use your journal to create word pictures that express your dreams and desires for your future. Focus on what you want, not what you don't want. Try out different approaches:

- Free flowing, stream of consciousness writing, or just make lists addressing all of the aspects of what you imagine to be a full and balanced life.

- Use the following categories to trigger your thinking:
    - Career/Business
    - Physical Body/Health
    - Play/Enjoyment
    - Lifestyle
    - Creative Expression/Hobbies
    - Love Relationship/Life Partner
    - Children/Family
    - Pets
    - Extended Family
    - Friends
    - Spirituality/Religion
    - Emotional Well-being
    - Personal Growth/Learning
    - Home Environment
    - Travel/Vacations
    - Prosperity/Wealth
    - Fame/Recognition
    - Service/Contributions
    - Anything else that is important to you!

- Try a creative writing approach: be the star in your own movie script, write a story called "A Day in the Life."

- Try a structured writing approach: answer the following questions about each of your desires:

  What do I want?

  Why do I want it? What are the benefits of having it?

  Why do I believe I can be, do, or have it?

- Declare your desires out loud.

  - Find a trusted friend or hire a life coach who can witness your declaration and be a sounding board for your ideas and dreams and be a supportive presence for your efforts to move forward.

  - If there isn't anyone you feel comfortable sharing your dreams with, find a place you can be in solitude and declare your desires out loud. Say it with positive energy and conviction.

- Craft your personal vision statement.

  - Go back and read what you've written in your journal and look at the picture collage you have created.

  - From the above two sources, build a list of words and phrases that represent exciting aspects of who you are and who you are becoming; words that describe what you love and deeply value; words that describe what you desire and what you aspire to do with your life. Challenge yourself to fill an entire page or more with these descriptive words.

  - Spend a few moments to read and review your list and really enjoy the positive energy that emits from the page!

  - Now take this list and circle the ten or twenty words and phrases that are the most exciting and energizing to you.

- Write your short list of words on a new piece of paper. These are the primary words and phrases you'll want to incorporate in your personal vision statement; however, you are not limited to only these words.

- Using the above short list of words, craft a sentence-or-two statement, starting with the words "I am" that captures the essence of who you are. Then add on a sentence starting with the words, "My purpose is…" that expresses what you desire to do with your life. Take your time and don't expect to get it right on the first try. Keep playing with it, scratch out and start over as many times as needed until you feel you have created a statement that has real energy for you. When you can say "YES!" with gusto, you will have a compelling personal vision statement.

- Read your personal vision statement several times a day, particularly first thing in the morning and at night before you go to bed. Post it where you will see it often as a constant reminder of who you are and where you are going.

Stepping Stone Six:
Harnessing the Power of Intention
Creating an inspiring life plan

Visit www.GiveWingsToYourDreams.com to request a free template for creating your life plan.

- Choose the building blocks for your life plan.
  - Think of your life as a pie containing eight segments. Draw a pie of your life on a piece of paper. Pick a label for each segment that best captures the eight most important aspects of your life right now, or the aspects that need the most attention to create a quality of life that inspires you.

- Ask yourself, "If all these aspects of my life are working, will I have a satisfying life?" If not, keep revising your pie until the picture of your life feels complete.

♦ Create an intention statement for each segment identified above.
- Before crafting each intention statement, ask yourself the following questions about this segment of your life plan:

> What do I want to do, be, or have?
>
> How do I want to go about achieving it?
>
> How will I feel when I have achieved it?

- With the answers to the above questions in mind, begin drafting your intention statement. Start with the words, "I am…" or "My intention is to…" Remember to "act as if" when crafting this statement as it becomes a mini-vision statement for the new reality you want to create for yourself.

- Now, for this intention statement, create a list of choices and actions you will make in order to carry out your intention.

> My Choices:
>
> Ask yourself, "Now that I am clear about my intention for _____, what choices will I make in daily life to ensure that I am on track with this intention?
>
> My Commitment to Action:
>
> List actions in support of the above choices, that are specific and measurable, that you are willing to commit to in the coming days, weeks, or months

- Repeat this process until you have completed your intention statements, choices, and commitment to action for all eight of the segments of your pie of life.

- Use your life plan to evaluate new opportunities and requests for your time.
  - Does this decision fit with the vision and intentions I hold for my life?
  - If I make this choice, will it further my progress toward the future I envision?

- Review your life plan on a regular basis to keep your focus clear and your energy charged. Revisit your intention statements once a year and your choices and actions monthly if not weekly to keep your plan current. Treat this as a living document to guide your life on an ongoing basis.

Stepping Stone Seven:
Staying True to Your Vision
Navigating the bumps in the road

- Be gentle with yourself. Practice patience. Value the baby steps and allow your plan to unfold at a pace that works for you. With time and focus, you will get where you want to go.

- Focus on creating one new habit at a time. Pick the most important or impactful habit and integrate it into your life. Experience some success with this one new habit, then add another. Experience some success with two new habits, then add another, etc.

- Give yourself status reports.
  - Schedule a "staff meeting" with yourself, once a week at the same time, on the same day each week.

  - Reaffirm your vision, review your life plan, assess your progress and plan your next steps.

  - Keep your weekly status report simple:

    Review of Last Week:
    - Wins/Accomplishments/Insights:
    - Challenges and Obstacles:
    - What needs attention?

    Plan for Next Week:
    - What do I want to accomplish?
    - What are my top three priorities for the week?
    - What will I do to take care of myself?

  - Set reasonable expectations and keep the commitments you make to yourself.

  - Acknowledge your progress and celebrate your wins!

  - Keep your progress reports in a file or a binder for easy access, to review and remind yourself how far you have come.

- Optional daily status report:
  - If you have difficulty maintaining focus, try this daily structure in addition to your weekly status reports. These can be done at the beginning or end of each day.

    Regarding Yesterday (or Today)
    - What worked?
    - What didn't work?
    - Insights:

Preparing for Today (or Tomorrow)
- What three things do I want to accomplish?
- What actions will ensure balance and well-being?
- Other To Do items to capture for later:

♦ Consider hiring a life coach to help you:
- Work through the Stepping Stone process
- Clarify your vision and purpose
- Create your life plan
- Stay on track and keep moving forward

♦ Consider starting a support group/study group to work through the Stepping Stones and support each other in moving forward. To download guidelines for setting up a study group, visit www.GiveWingsToYourDreams.com.
- Create some ground rules
  Listen without judgment
  Offer suggestions without attachment
  Use empowering language
  Leave negativity at the door
  Have fun!

♦ Consider joining the on-line support community at www.GiveWingsToYourDreams.com

♦ Revisit the Stepping Stones
- If you find yourself tired or facing a new kind of turmoil, revisit Stepping Stone One and recommit to your self-care and nurturing.

- If you find yourself feeling stuck and having trouble moving forward, revisit Stepping Stone Three, and take a look to see if your inner critic might be engaging in self-sabotage tactics.

- If you find you have slipped away from joyful anticipation and into frustration and negative expectation, revisit Stepping Stone Four and reconnect with ways to find joy in the journey.

- If you find yourself moving at top speed and implementing your life plan with ease, you may want to revisit Stepping Stone Six on a frequent basis to challenge yourself to create new and even more exciting intentions for yourself.

- Again, practice patience. Make a commitment to stay true to your vision, to navigate the bumps in the road and get back on track, to seek out support and use the tools provided to keep you focused and moving forward. Celebrate your wins and enjoy the unfolding of your new life!

I'd love to hear your story!

I would love to hear how reading *Give Wings To Your Dreams* and working the Stepping Stone process has enabled you to reawaken your joy and passion for life! Please visit www.GiveWingsToYour Dreams.com to share your story and your contact information. With your permission, I may use your story in a future book! I look forward to hearing from you!

Additional Tools and Support

Join the Give Wings To Your Dreams Community

Visit www.GiveWingsToYourDreams.com to join our on-line support community! It's a way to meet and interact with other women who are on a similar journey and to gain access to additional tools, resources, inspiration and connections to further your journey. When you join our community you will:

- Make new friends as you support each other to stay true to your vision and take productive steps toward fulfilling your dreams.

- Participate in phone conference calls designed to educate, inspire, and empower you to get more of what you want in life.

- Access our resource library that includes a free life plan template to make it easier for you to capture your Inspired Life Design on paper.

- Receive ongoing inspirational tips, ideas, quotes, stories and advice to enhance your life by subscribing to the Give Wings to Your Dreams e-mail newsletter.

To join, please visit www.GiveWingsToYourDreams.com

Helpful Books and Websites

I have put together a list of books, websites and other resources that I think you will find helpful on your journey and will offer you practical tools, support and inspiration. Many of the items listed are ones that have helped me personally in my own life. All are resources that I routinely recommend to my clients. Because I am continually adding to this list, and I want you to have up-to-date access to these recommendations, I am offering this information on my community website. Here you will find a list of books and websites on topics such as:

- Life Transitions
- Starting a Business
- Relationships
- Manifesting Your Desires
- Health
- Emotional Well-being
- Feng Shui
- Therapy

- Career Exploration
- Creative Expression
- Prosperity
- Personal Growth
- Weight Loss
- Getting Organized
- Life Coaching
- And More!

Please visit www.GiveWingsToYourDreams.com to explore these resources.

Deepen Your Exploration with the Give Wings To Your Dreams Companion Workbook

Give Wings To Your Dreams: Personal Journal and Activity Guide

A workbook format to guide you through the Give Wings to Your Dreams Seven Stepping Stone process. Includes additional questions and activities to support you on your journey.

To order, please visit www.GoldenWingsPress.com.

Life Choice Retreats of Santa Barbara with Lauren Sullivan

An Empowering, Life Changing Experience for Women Who Want More Balance, Joy, and Passion in Life

"Nobody's ever paid this much attention to me! I felt deeply heard, nurtured, inspired and empowered. I had never taken this kind of time just for me before. It's an investment that has paid for itself many times over."

–Life Choice Retreats Client

In the beautiful resort city of Santa Barbara, California, also known as the *American Riviera*, **Life Choice Retreats** gives you the rare experience of taking time out to immerse yourself in an intensive exploration that's *all about you and only you*. Your retreat experience will be one-on-one with the focus on helping you to find yourself and a new and exciting vision and purpose for your life. You will leave with your own Inspired Life Design—a life plan that will energize you and reawaken your joy and passion for life.

Group retreat programs are also available. For more information, visit: www.InspiredLifeDesign.com

Contact Information

For access to more resources and to support you on your journey through the Give Wings to Your Dreams Seven Stepping Stone process, please visit: **www.GiveWingsToYourDreams.com**.

To order additional books, workbooks, audio programs and other inspirational products, please visit: **www.GoldenWingsPress.com**.

To contact Lauren Sullivan for more information on her coaching and retreat programs, for media inquiries, or to book her for a speaking engagement, please visit: **www.InspiredLifeDesign.com**.

Acknowledgements

To Carol McClelland, Ph.D., author of *The Seasons of Change*, and my original role model for coaching women through transitions. Who knew that twelve years ago when I wandered into that breakfast meeting to hear you speak, that our paths would cross so many times and in so many ways? I will always remember your Sea Ranch retreat as a pivotal turning point in my life. If my work can impact others lives the way yours has impacted mine, I will be truly honored.

To Sylvia Murray—you saw me writing a book nearly a decade ago when it seemed out of the realm of possibility for me. Your joyful, loving and positive visions helped me hold the space for a better future when I couldn't visualize it for myself. Your words of inspiration kept me buoyed through many challenging moments in my life. Thank you for shining your light to help me find my way.

To Mary Lord for taking me through Julia Cameron's, *The Artist's Way* book, in a workshop that opened the doors again to joyful creative expression, an accomplishment for which my inner child will be eternally grateful.

To Jacquelyn Aldana and *The 15-Minute Miracle*® books and playshops for introducing me to the power and importance of consciously choosing positive feeling in order to manifest what you really want in life.

To Fran Fisher, The Academy for Coach Training and LYV Enterprises, Inc. in Bellevue, Washington for the training, certification and licensing programs that have given me so many skills and tools that have enabled me to become a powerful life coach and retreat facilitator. *Give Wings To Your Dreams* was born out of the personal vision your programs guided me to create for myself.

To the Unity Church, particularly Rev. Stan Hampson and Rev. Linda Spencer for providing a safe haven for spiritual exploration in a warm, loving and tolerant environment and offering wonderful support and encouragement for those on a journey from lost to found.

To the many authors whose work has inspired me to stretch my wings and grow over the years, especially: Susan Jeffers, Ph.D., Daphne Rose Kingma, Cheryl Richardson, Debbie Ford, Catherine Ponder, Jerry and Esther Hicks, Jon Kabat-Zinn, Oriah Mountain Dreamer, Sonia Choquette, Ph.D., Charlotte Kasl, Ph.D., and Julia Cameron.

To the many coaches who have offered their help and support along the way. I would like to acknowledge all of you for your contributions to my growth, especially: Margie Summerscales Heiler, MCC, Vikki Brock, MCC, and Laura Jensen Shope. The three of you have been instrumental in helping me to carry my vision forward. I would also like to acknowledge my very special coaching support group—Darcy, Teddy, and Andrea for cheering me on at the earliest stages of my coaching career.

To Jack Barnard and Lee Glickstein, for teaching me the art of storytelling, for encouraging me to allow my authentic self to shine through on stage, and for helping me achieve my dream to become an inspirational speaker.

To the Santa Barbara Writers Conference and especially Cork Millner, author of *Write from the Start,* for recognizing my talent with an "Excellence in Writing" award in 2003. To literary agents, Nancy Ellis-Bell and Michael Larsen for offering your feedback, suggestions and encouragement to keep going with my project. To the members of my writers group, especially Gina Rae Hendrickson and Maggie Dennison, for reading my early drafts, and providing me with helpful and constructive feedback. To my friends and clients who took the time to read my manuscript before going to press and offering your loving and enthusiastic support!

To Jan B. King, Executive Director of the eWomenPublishingNetwork for serving as the midwife in the final stages of writing this book, for providing your honest and direct feedback, and for guiding me productively through the maze of the publishing world.

To all of the talented women who have providing their professional expertise at various stages of creating and marketing my book, especially: Gloria Balcom, Nancy Marriott, Christine Frank, Dawn Putney, Sherry Hoesly, and Peg Booth.

To Meganne Forbes, an infinitely talented artist, who put her heart and soul into creating the perfect painting to grace the cover of this book.

To my clients, each and every one of you have enriched my life. Your stories offer inspiration to my readers—I know they can relate to your experiences. Thank you for trusting me and allowing me to share in your journey.

To my long-time friends, Sharon Kerr, Linda Brewer, and Roseanne Duncan, for being such good listeners and for being my lifeline in my time of intense turmoil. To my Santa Barbara friends—there are too many of you to name—for welcoming me to the community with open arms, supporting my endeavors, and helping me to feel at home so quickly. To the loving memory of Roseanne and Deborah, you continue to touch my life.

To the many professionals who have helped me to heal physically and emotionally, especially: Carol McDonald, Marty Klein, Lawrence Epstein, Nathan Becker, Beth McDonald, Mary Tingaud, and Mia Lunden.

To my ex-husband (who wishes to remain anonymous) for continuing to be my friend and for being there for the kids. I acknowledge the enormous personal strength, resilience, courage, and tenacity it took to overcome your addiction and its associated challenges, and to move on productively in life.

To my parents, Jack and Sybil Butler, role models for two people who accept each other "just the way you are." You've been married over sixty years! There should be an award for that! To my Dad, a veteran of World War II who endured unimaginable horrors, serving our country with great honor, and survived to bring our family into being. To my mother, a Rice University graduate, who chose to stay home with the kids, always striving to give us the very best foundation in life. To my sisters, Mary Tarver and Beverly Wright, my very best friends and mentors. I've learned so much from both of you! To my extended family, some who live as far away as Germany, I'm glad you are a part of my life. To the Sullivan family, for embracing me as one of your own.

To my husband, Eric Sullivan and my sons, Greg and Kevin, for tolerating my long stretches of intense writing that brought this book into being. Thank you for your patience and unwavering support, and for believing in me!

About the Author

*"Her intuitive insights reached to the depths of my soul,
skillfully guiding me to transform fear and doubt
into positive and fulfilling plans, actions and outcomes."*

–Retreat Client

Lauren Sullivan speaks from her heart and personal experience, as an insightful life coach, a riveting speaker and an award-winning writer. Lauren is a former high-tech marketing executive who embarked on her own major life and career transition at the age of forty.

At the pinnacle of her career, personal trauma, triggered by her ex-husband's drug addiction, turned her life into a crisis of fear, despair, and extreme burnout. Hitting rock bottom became her catalyst to embark on a healing journey that led her to new beginnings and a passionate sense of purpose. She is a life coach who has truly walked her talk.

Lauren made the powerful choice to follow her dream—to make a difference in the lives of women—by openly sharing her story, her wisdom, and her Seven Stepping Stones to reawaken your joy and passion for life.

As a professional coach, Lauren received her formal training at the Academy for Coach Training in Bellevue, Washington and is certified through the International Coach Federation.

Lauren facilitates intensive private and small group retreat programs that guide women to become the architects of their own life designs. Her retreat programs culminate in the creation of unique and compelling personal vision statements and inspiring life plans for each participant. Her focus is to assist clients in making work/life choices that will create a rich and robust quality of life.

As an inspirational speaker, Lauren is available for keynotes, panels and private workshops. She speaks frequently to large women's groups, bringing her audience to silence, tears and joy as she shares her dramatic story and engages them in an inspirational journey to a place of hope and possibility.

As a writer, Lauren received an "Excellence in Writing" award for non-fiction from the prestigious Santa Barbara Writers Conference.

Prior to discovering her own joyful life purpose, Lauren spent over fifteen years successfully climbing her career ladder in the Silicon Valley fast lane while working with industry giants Hewlett-Packard, Sun Microsystems, and Cisco Systems. She holds a Bachelor of Science degree in Technology from the University of Houston.

After eight years as a single mother raising two boys on her own, Lauren recently remarried. She lives, writes, coaches, and facilitates intensive retreats in the beautiful resort city of Santa Barbara, California.

To contact Lauren Sullivan for information on her coaching and retreat programs, or to book her for a speaking engagement, please visit: www.InspiredLifeDesign.com.